Cosmic Ordering
for Beginners

The Mohr Method

Cosmic Ordering for Beginners
The Mohr Method

Barbel Mohr
& Clemens Maria Mohr

HAY HOUSE

Australia • Canada • Hong Kong • India
South Africa • United Kingdom • United States

First published and distributed in the United Kingdom by:
Hay House UK Ltd, 292B Kensal Rd, London W10 5BE. Tel.: (44) 20 8962 1230;
Fax: (44) 20 8962 1239. www.hayhouse.co.uk

Published and distributed in the United States of America by:
Hay House, Inc., PO Box 5100, Carlsbad, CA 92018-5100. Tel.: (1) 760 431 7695 or (800) 654
5126; Fax: (1) 760 431 6948 or (800) 650 5115. www.hayhouse.com

Published and distributed in Australia by:
Hay House Australia Ltd, 18/36 Ralph St, Alexandria NSW 2015. Tel.: (61) 2 9669 4299;
Fax: (61) 2 9669 4144. www.hayhouse.com.au

Published and distributed in the Republic of South Africa by:
Hay House SA (Pty), Ltd, PO Box 990, Witkoppen 2068. Tel./Fax: (27) 11 467 8904.
www.hayhouse.co.za

Published and distributed in India by:
Hay House Publishers India, Muskaan Complex, Plot No.3, B-2, Vasant Kunj, New Delhi –
110 070. Tel.: (91) 11 4176 1620; Fax: (91) 11 4176 1630. www.hayhouse.co.in

Distributed in Canada by:
Raincoast, 9050 Shaughnessy St, Vancouver, BC V6P 6E5. Tel.: (1) 604 323 7100;
Fax: (1) 604 323 2600

The authors of this book do not dispense medical advice or prescribe the use of any technique as
a form of treatment for physical or medical problems without the advice of a physician, either
directly or indirectly. The intent of the authors is only to offer information of a general nature to
help you in your quest for emotional and spiritual wellbeing. In the event you use any of the
information in this book for yourself, which is your constitutional right, the authors and the
publisher assume no responsibility for your actions.

A catalogue record for this book is available from the British Library.

Previously published as *Die Mohr Methode* by KOHA-Verlag GmbH, Burgrain, 2005,
ISBN 3-936862-62-1

Translated by: Dennis McAllister, Nick Handforth. www.citylanguages.de

ISBN 978-1-4019-1551-3

Printed and bound in Great Britain by TJ International, Padstow, Cornwall.

Contents

☆ **Introduction** ☆

Dear readers,

When I wrote *The Cosmic Ordering Service*, I never ever thought it could become a real book. And even when I did eventually find a publishing house, after having distributed many photocopies of the text, the publisher still said we would be very lucky if we sold 5000 copies.

So I figured this book would never be read by anyone outside the 'spiritual scene', so it was a big surprise for everyone when, in 2005, we passed a million copies sold.

It brought in quite a lot of questions from people who were wondering whether I was a little mad, because they had never heard of anything like this before.

For example: why should 'ordering' something from the cosmos work? How do expectations influence my daily life?

Not everybody knows about the power of the subconscious and how it secretly leads us through life.

So this book is written for all those who want to know a little more about the basics.

Let me just explain one of these 'basics of ordering from the cosmos' as an example. If you expect everything in your life to be difficult, it will be. Your thoughts and feelings are like a command to your subconscious. Out of all the opportunities in life, it sees only the difficult ones and constantly misses the easy ones.

Now, if you WISH for something else, your subconscious belief about wishes is probably that they work sometimes and sometimes not.

But if you order something, your subconscious, as crazy as it may sound, says: 'We order something? All right, I know that word and I know that what we [you and it] order does usually come…' And so without further reprogramming of the subconscious, or difficult yoga exercises, the new expectation is already there.

Immediately your subconscious starts to watch out for fitting opportunities to your 'order'. Suddenly it sees the things it has been blind to before. It is a little trick we play with ourselves.

How this works exactly is explained in this book.

And when does the cosmic magic come in? As soon as you really get started! We are all interconnected. Quantum physicists know that we are all one on a subatomic level. Mostly we do not know how that applies in our daily life. But it does as soon as you start to feel connected to everything that is. That is when you draw into your life like magic all the things that you really want.

Nature is interested in happy people because happy people who really lead a fulfilled life respect nature. And even Einstein said that all nature tends towards harmony. So all you need to do is to let your real nature come through.

Natural happiness for you,

Barbel Mohr

☆ **What is the Mohr Method ?** ☆

The Mohr Method is a system of building-blocks which anybody can use to reprogramme their inner automatisms in exactly the way they want. We're long past the idea that one person should play the guru, explaining that only they have found the one true way to contact the inner light, and that this is the right way for everyone else.

The modern method is that each person should develop their own way, based on a foundation of enlightened and inspiring knowledge. When Barbel Mohr met Clemens Maria Mohr for the first time, she greatly enjoyed his way of teaching as he brings this precise foundation of enlightening and inspiring knowledge. This makes it so easy to understand, analytically and logically, even for very rational people, that it will reward them for their entire lives if they apply themselves to their mental powers!

Clemens, on the other hand, who had until then focused mainly on business and the economy, was attracted by Barbel's light style and her application of her findings in the private sphere.

They therefore offer methods which can be applied to both one's private life and in business. The reader is encouraged to take the first step to becoming master of themselves by using the yin–yang approach to set up their own method within themselves. The Mohr Method gives you the building-blocks and you are more than welcome to use these to put together your very own, individualised method.

How it all began for Barbel Mohr

All of you who have already read books by me, Barbel Mohr, know how it all began for me. For those who don't, here's a short summary.

Friends tried to convince me that the powers of thought and of the unconscious were to be taken seriously. Just to prove that this was all hocus-pocus, I undertook an experiment and failed miserably as, to my shock, the attempt was successful. What I had asked for came to be, just as ordered. 'Help! Save me!' was my first reaction, then, 'Hurray, a never-ending cornucopia!' was my second.

What followed were many trips around the world, further experiments, visits to spiritual teachers, mind training and the testing of my new-found knowledge from every angle.

I saw that miracles were indeed possible. There were too many for me to refuse to believe in them and simply to ignore them. But just knowing that something is possible didn't mean that I'd be able to do it myself. This is the unfortunate mistake that many in the esoteric scene make.

Let me put it this way: if you had grown up in the most isolated spot on earth and had never heard of tightrope walking, somersaults or juggling, you would believe them to be magic or witchcraft when someone told you about them. If a circus were then to come by, you would see it in person and think, 'Aha! It is possible.' But would you be able to copy it? No, not by a long shot.

We are all still very much in the dark when it comes to what science knows about the powers of the mind. It is great when we at least realise that our spirit is capable of 'juggling, tightrope walking or somersaults'. You need further practice before you can become a master yourself and give your spirit clear instructions as to exactly what kind of somersault you want to make (success in your professional life, your private life, or for your health).

We have written this book to make this as simple as possible and the Mohr Method accessible even to the most rational people.

I wish you much joy and success in this journey into your own spiritual sources and exploration of your powers.

Barbel Mohr

And how did it all begin for Clemens Maria Mohr?

The setting sun shone over my shoulder from behind, illuminating the words which held me spellbound as no book had done before. It was not particularly unusual for me to be poring over a book for hours; what was unusual was that the sun was shining on me on the balcony of my parents-in-law's house – 300 kilometres away from home.

In the middle of the biggest family get-together – relatives had arrived from every corner of Germany for the Hohentweil festival in Singen – someone was sitting tucked away in a corner, not taking part in any conversation, only replying curtly when asked a question, and then sticking his nose purposefully back between the pages of print. All this although he only sees the rest of the family once or twice a year on special occasions or, as on this occasion, for the traditional castle festival on Table Mountain by Lake Constance.

No, it wasn't to escape the traditional family event – these are normally far too entertaining for that. It was a truly deep interest in what was for me a completely new field. I was fascinated.

I grew up in a Catholic household with strong connections to the church. My father was the secretary of the church society, in addition to his day job. Naturally the whole family supported him in this. My mother washed the church robes for the pastor and we children were servers at mass, general errand boys and always at the ready should we be needed.

This close relationship faded rapidly with increasing age and maturity. For me the teachings of the church had too little connection to real life, those of the church leaders too little to do with those of 'the man on the street'.

Help in life was needed, but not given. This led me to separate myself strictly from ideas of God, Jesus and even from faith itself. I well remember the moment when I was almost shocked to realise that I didn't believe in anything any more.

And then along came this book!

My belief in the world and my faith seemed to revive in the shortest of times. If not to the extent of where it is today, given the circumstances at the time, quite dramatically.

A certain Dr Joseph Murphy, at the time a completely unknown American for me, explained in the book that we have a state inside us called the unconscious which is important and guides us in many ways through life, and that we programme this unconscious through our thoughts. We are what we think. According to Dr Murphy, the foundation for our entire lives, whether for health, happiness, success, material comfort or partnerships, is our thoughts. We decide what happens to us, and no one else. He also sees the unconscious as a synonym for God, the power that creates us.

'Faith can move mountains,' as it says in the Bible.

This immediately set all the bells in my head ringing wildly. 'How stupid!' I thought. You go to school for years, study, work, gain experience and then someone comes along and tells you that the only thing you have to do is to think straight. This was just a little bit too simple! Or was it? The idea was almost too simple to be made-up. And with every sentence that I read, with every page I devoured, the certainty within me grew: this was it! Thought is the basis. We are completely responsible for ourselves! We live our lives through the way in which we think. I was hooked.

In the breaks in which I was forced to stop reading for meals, so as not to completely ruin the family get-together, they asked what I was reading and I spoke enthusiastically about what I had just learned. The whole thing was as new for everyone at the table as it was for me. Perhaps it was the way I explained it, as the reaction was either reserved ('Yes, and?') or outright rejection. One particular brother-in-law was clearly at the stage I had been at just a few pages and paragraphs before, as his reaction was, 'What nonsense!'

Then the signal was given for us all to set off. 'What now?' I thought, but then I remembered, between the possibility of having wishes fulfilled and of attaining perfect health, the real reason for our visit: 'Oh yes, the Hohentwiel festival.' Just to explain, the Hohentwiel is a table mountain complete with a ruined castle from the Middle Ages in which a fantastic festival takes place every summer. Needless to say, this attracts countless people. We set off, with children and prams and all of the things a travelling clan needs, with me feeling a slight melancholia. I had left the book at home as I didn't want to test the patience of my family any further.

To avoid total chaos at the festival, the little mountain is closed to traffic throughout the festival, with buses bringing the masses to the top. Picture the scene: every few minutes a bus would arrive, and before it could come to a complete standstill and the doors open properly, the crowd would surge forward with a steely determination, pushing, shoving and squeezing itself onto the bus until, overloaded, the doors would shut, at which time a few poor souls would realise that they hadn't quite made it and were still outside or even stuck between the doors. And there we were, in the middle of all of this, with a pram!

After our repeated attempts at boarding had failed, since cumbersome baggage doesn't help at all, my brother-in-law said to me in a peevish tone, suited to the situation, 'Go on, use that positive thinking of yours, make the bus stop here and open its doors right in front of us!'

I felt a bit put off by the hopelessness of the situation, and added to that, I was only a beginner! I had only heard about the method a few hours before and was already expected to perform miracles. Really, what was I supposed to do?

On the one hand, I saw the chaos surrounding me, on the other I felt my pride under attack, so I began to think of a way of making the impossible possible. I didn't want to give in! And then I had an idea. The buses had to turn near to where we were standing, and face up the hill to let the crowds board, so while one of the buses was turning, I ran over to the driver and explained our somewhat bulky baggage situation. And bingo! I couldn't suppress a smile (in reality I laughed like a hyena) as the bus stopped right at the spot my brother-in-law had wished for. The power of thought? I was astounded myself! Was this really to be attributed to my thoughts? I had, after all, actually spoken to the driver, but this didn't change the fact that I had thought about it and that it had then come true.

The path that one takes to reach the goal, which I was later to understand more clearly, is secondary, and anyway there was no question of hocus-pocus, nor even of flying pigs. Had I not thought about it, I would never have had the idea.

This really was my first experience of success in using the method, and from that moment on, the subject just wouldn't leave me alone. The model used by Dr Joseph Murphy, however, seemed to me to be a bit too simple in many respects. The basic premise was fascinating, but was lacking supporting explanation, or rather it seemed to me that the explanation he offered was neither exact nor scientific enough. I wanted something more logical. I had recently completed a degree in sports science and had explored the well-known field of mental training in sports psychology in detail. Were there any connections? There were without a doubt, but how were these to be explained and what was behind it all?

I wanted to get to the bottom of these questions. I would like to present my findings to you, who are reading this book as little by coincidence as I had come to read *The Power of the Unconscious Mind* by Dr Joseph Murphy.

In the meantime, I have made a career out of it. As I write this in 2005, I have been a management trainer for more than 15 years, specialising in the fields of motivation and personal development. Once I had fully investigated the scientific causes, it was relatively easy to teach these to people and above all to give them clear instructions on how to put them into practice in their daily lives.

The upshot was that, even given the fairly narrow goals that businesses often set themselves, only a clear approach can really guarantee long-term success.

Just one more thing in advance: please choose the things from this book which seem useful to you. Then combine these with your current approach to life. I don't want to offer you a ready-made meal, but rather to teach you the basics of cooking so that you will be able to prepare your favourite dish whenever you like.

Let me take a metaphor from my colleague Vera F. Birkenbihl – view this book as a supermarket. All of the ideas which I put forward here are products lining the shelves of the supermarket. You have a big shopping cart and can fill it with anything you like and then take it all with you. You can, however, also leave other things on the shelves.

I myself took a long time before I put everything into my cart, so I can well understand it if you want to leave the odd thing sitting on the shelves. The important thing is that you know where to find it again. Perhaps you will walk through the aisles some time later and pick up something new. The best thing is that everything that you take with you has already been paid for, so you can go ahead and fill up the cart! You can only gain from it!

Clemens Maria Mohr

The Mohrs

… are, by the way, related to each other in spirit, which is why we have chosen to write this book together. There is no further family relationship between us, in spite of the name we share.

☆ The Conscious and the Subconscious ☆

As a motivational coach and success trainer, I (Clemens) am often asked why the mind is so important to my work. Why am I occupied with 'thought' instead of 'action'? It would make more sense to negotiate, sell or lead and motivate your co-workers successfully than to just think successfully!

I (Barbel) also find that during the breaks at seminars and presentations there's often the objection that the whole 'positive thoughts' thing isn't really usable if you put it into action afterward. That's surely true, but there is a small flaw in that way of thinking. You can't even move your little finger without thinking. Besides that, and we'll look at this soon, positive thoughts alone, which we just force ourselves to have, will produce nothing.

Basically everything,
down to the smallest thing,
is a thought.

Everything we do requires at least a single thought. We can't even place one foot in front of the other without thinking about it; if not consciously, then at least unconsciously.

Everything we say requires at least a single thought (even when it doesn't seem like it with some people!).

Everything our five senses perceive – sight, sound, smell, taste and touch – isn't just funnelled into us, but analysed by us.

Everything that we perceive is processed into thoughts, and these are what are saved.

Everything that exists today has required at least a single thought. Every object, every project has sprung from an existing idea. And from this idea, from this thought, a plan was made and only then was it realised.

If no one had stopped and thought that carrying heavy objects around on their shoulders was strenuous, the wheel would have never been thought of. We still don't, as they say, know what came first, the chicken or the egg. It is clear, though, that with any invention the idea, the thought, came first.

In the same way you can make new inventions for yourself if you want new working conditions, private relationships or better health. Most people never achieve their goals, because they don't have any. They sit in front of the television at night and watch the achievements of people with clear goals. And then they sit there asking themselves why their lives aren't successful like those people on the box. After all, they have been trying so hard.

I'll let you in on a secret. They are straining to carry heavy things around on their shoulders. The successful people on the box, however, whom they occasionally envy, have invented a wheel for themselves and for their lives. And to do this, a thought was first required! Those who don't act on the knowledge that thoughts steer our lives will never invent a wheel.

The people whom we initially envy are not always worth envying, though. People who only think of career success and ignore their private lives won't be much happier than those sitting around in front of the television.

Don't be satisfied with simple wheels. Invent double and triple wheels for your career, health and private life! We'll see how to do this a little later.

Even our feelings, which normally come 'from the gut', are really just thoughts. When we think about certain things or receive important news, we process all of these things through thought and then react with feelings.

> *Everything that exists*
> *was originally a thought.*

This is why it makes sense to concentrate on the mind. You'll then be able to correct all these other areas in one fell swoop!

While we're on the subject of 'thinking', we have to look at the human spirit, the psyche, which produces these thoughts.

This human spirit is split, as it were, into two areas. The first is that which we call reason or logic. It contains the rational logic that manoeuvres us through life in how we perceive things, assess them, reach logical conclusions and well-considered decisions. Reason has been hard-won within our society. We're proud of this; we raise our children from an early age to 'think logically' and even divide society into different classes according to how rationally they think.

At the top are the academics whom we may put on pedestals because they seem to possess more 'reason' than others.

It doesn't really matter how well these people cope with life or what their quality of life is, if they're happy or unhappy, satisfied or dissatisfied. Just the fact that they are able to think logically puts them above the rest of the world.

The things that we process in this part of our psyche are 'known' to us, and form our 'knowledge'.

On the other hand, there are clearly parts to our psyche that we don't know very much about. We approach the part beyond the conscious with a bit of difficulty. These parts lie below the conscious as if covered up, so we'll call these parts the 'subconscious'.

The subconscious is much larger than the conscious.

To put it graphically, our psyche is very similar to an iceberg, with the conscious above the waterline and the subconscious below.

The subconscious performs various tasks that are vital to people. For one, the subconscious saves all the information that we, no matter how, have received. Modern hypnosis research, in fact, has proven that everything we have ever experienced in our lives (seen, heard, done, said or even thought) is saved in our subconscious. Nothing is lost. The question of memory (and its division into long-, middle-, short- and ultra-short-term) isn't a question of whether or not information is stored, but of how we access it.

A person can in fact remember things under hypnosis that they have long 'forgotten', down to the smallest detail. Unbelievable but true. It's an amazing storeroom.

Let me (Clemens) share with you something that happened at one of my seminars. While talking about hypnosis, a participant told us of his then 15-year-old son who had major health problems. They had gone from doctor to doctor and no one could really help him. That is, until they were with a therapist who put the boy under hypnosis. While under hypnosis, the boy recalled what he had got for his first birthday, what clothes he had on and who was there. There was no way he could have known this information from stories or from anywhere else! Naturally, the father was completely surprised and checked the boy's story with photos, the boy's grandmother and other people who had been present.

This is a good example of how everything is in fact saved in the subconscious.

Some tasks that we need often in life function automatically. These are known as automatisms, and we have a whole series of such automatisms saved within us. All of our internal bodily functions, for example, are automatically run this way by our nervous system. Circulation, breathing and digestion are clear examples of this.

> *If we consciously had to take our next breath,*
> *we'd surely be long extinct.*

A further series of so-called base needs is found within us. These were described in the form of a hierarchy by the American psychologist Abraham Harold Maslow in 1968.

At the lowest level are the base physiological needs such as nourishment (eating and drinking), breathing, shelter, sleep and sexuality. This is about real 'basic survival' for individuals as well as society as a whole.

If we didn't have even one of these things, we would die; first as individuals and in the end all of humanity.

At the second level is the need for safety and security. When survival needs are taken care of at the first level, humanity wants to be able to fulfil these needs in as much safety as possible.

This need for safety goes far beyond the bodily, though. We want to know who we are, for example, in comparison to others. We want to know how we should or are allowed to behave, especially in unfamiliar social groups or countries. We want to be secure in knowing what effect a certain mental immobility we get with increasing age will have on us. We want to hold onto the past by any means possible, for safety's sake. We also want to secure our future, which is why we feel the need for savings and insurance.

The third level shows social and affiliation needs. People have always formed clans, and during our development and life we have always relied on the relevant group. Young children who are only able to fulfil their basic bodily needs aren't able to survive. Without direct contact with others they die.

Nowadays organisations and clubs are created to satisfy these needs, seeing as how the extended family, at least in our society, often no longer exists as a social unit.

Important factors here are the possibility for communication and a feeling of security.

The fourth level, and this where it becomes interesting, shows self-esteem needs, the striving for acknowledgement, status, power and validation. If we're honest with ourselves, most of our goals lie in this area. There is, however, a distinctive feature that must be looked at:

As a rule, the first level, our physiological needs, is covered nowadays. At the second and third level there are very often deficiencies, which, when they can't be reconciled, manifest themselves in different ways.

One of these things is aggression; this is where we see screaming bosses, violent fathers and football hooligans.

In some people it manifests itself as depression, which is aggression turned inward. Drug abuse in every form, including cigarettes and alcohol, and suicide are often found in these cases.

The last and most common way of satisfying unfulfilled needs is mostly through compensation at this, the fourth level.

Some examples:

A man doesn't feel safe in his social environment and compensates for this by becoming a workaholic in order to get the recognition he desires from his company.

Someone else isn't sure what the future holds and feels insecure and so buys a safe car.

A woman feels an inner-emptiness in her life and compensates by binge shopping and eating.

Compensation is nothing unusual. Estimates show that almost two-thirds of the gross national product is spent on such compensatory things. This is comparable to the following situation.

You've got holes in your socks, and cold feet. It's much easier to reach the hole in your sweater, so you concentrate on that. But no matter how much you fix your sweater, you'll never have warm feet!

This brings us to the subject of self-esteem. Whether needs are met at the second or third levels depends to a great extent on our subjective viewpoint. The lower the manifestation of self-esteem, the higher the possible consequences. A person who loves themselves sufficiently doesn't need a status symbol in the garage to compensate for this love.

The clear recognition of individual needs and the fulfilment of these at the relevant level are prerequisites for leading a contented life. This is the only way that the fourth level can be mastered. If, however, new needs are constantly coming up from below, the fifth level will never be reached.

The fifth level is self-actualisation. The desire to actualise (realise) the self through one's own talents, goals, ideals and desires is a natural basic need. It lies deep within us and therefore must be taken into consideration. This isn't about the realisation of so-called recognition needs that belong to level four, though, but about things that we do for pure enjoyment. The pursuit of socially conscious careers (Mother Teresa being a star example) and the expression of an artistic talent whether in music or the visual arts are examples. (More on this later in the Goals chapter.)

The order in which we have to go through the Maslow hierarchy of needs always has to be from bottom to top: if we suffer from hunger, we'll never think about creating neighbourly relationships. And as long as we have problems with relationships, we'll never be able to realise our full potential. Many people are unable to achieve self-actualisation.

Around 90 per cent of our behaviour is subconsciously guided, which in turn is guided by our conscious thoughts!

Automatisms

Now we see further peculiarities of the subconscious: information that is received repeatedly is saved in the form of a model or automatism.

Repeated actions become automatisms.

Because it really does save everything, the subconscious can see when different pieces of information are repeatedly received. When something is repeated often enough, we 'learn' it and it is programmed as an automatism, which from then on more or less runs on its own. This is also proof that everything really is saved in the subconscious. If this information flowed through, like liquid through a sieve, then we'd never see that certain things had happened before. Everything would be new and we'd never learn anything!

We are all familiar with this process when we look at movement. A child who's just learning to walk has to make a conscious effort with each step. The more steps are made correctly, the more often the information is presented to the subconscious and the more the automatism is set, and a few days after mastering walking we ask ourselves if there was ever a time that the child couldn't walk.

The same goes for driving. When you began driving, how often did you have to concentrate on the brake, accelerator and clutch pedals, and the gears? How often do you have to now?

This automatism process is useful and sensible. Everything that we often need becomes entrenched so that we can keep our subconscious free for other things.

Imagine just an hour of your life where everything that you normally do has to be done consciously. Things like speaking, writing, calculating, moving, eating, drinking etc., etc., etc.!

You can test for yourself how automatically we move in many areas. Fold your arms. Now look at which arm is on top. The right or the left? It doesn't matter which of your arms is on top, but try doing it the other way round. The arm that's on top should now be on the bottom!

You have probably had the same problem with this test as most people. Some people think that it's impossible. You folded your arms in a certain way as a child, always repeating it until it happened automatically. You don't even think about it any more – it just happens automatically.

Or another example. Clasp your hands together. Which thumb is on top? The right or the left? Now unclasp your hands and try to clasp them again so that the other thumb is on top.

This exercise is also amazingly difficult. It shows, though, how deep-rooted some things are within us.

This process of automatism doesn't just work with our motor functions, but also in relation to our thoughts. Anything that we think often enough is saved in our subconscious as a model and as a consequence influences our behaviour.

Let's imagine that you have a neighbour who, in your opinion, behaves rather strangely. At least once a week while putting his car into his garage, he hits the wall – not hard, but he still does it. The strange thing is that he never gets upset. In the meantime, his car looks like it's been through a demolition derby and yet he doesn't seem very bothered by this. Strange!

If you see this enough times to become used to it and are still of the opinion that he's not quite right in the head, these thoughts have become an automatism. In the future, you'll no longer have to think that your neighbour's weird, you'll just know it. It'll become a part of your daily life and everything that you experience in connection to this neighbour will be judged under the basis of him being 'strange'. Whatever he does, he'll have no chance of being judged fairly by you.

Your behaviour towards him in the future will automatically be on this 'strange' basis. How you speak to him, your choice of words, your gestures and body language, your intonation are set with regard to him.

At least until another frequent action of your neighbour happens and erases the old programme.

Every frequently occurring thought is likewise saved as an automatism. And so this is a core point in our lives. A further point, besides the frequency of the thoughts that lead to an automatism in the subconscious, is their intensity, their emotional connection. Experiences that are connected to very strong emotions can become models after a single occurrence.

The classic example here is a child and a hot stove. Burnt fingers are so connected to terrible pain (an especially negative type of feeling) that a child doesn't have to touch the stove ten times to learn that it's hot. The associated feeling is as a rule so strong that once is enough.

Or let's look at the dramatic experience of the rape of a woman. The woman to whom this happens is almost always under enormous emotional strain. This can lead to an immediate emotional model: that all men are bad, for example. This imprint can shape her relationship to men for her whole life. Even if she consciously thinks that she has got over the experience, her subconscious will still always react with the same corresponding imprint.

In most cases, we humans don't behave consciously, that is we don't take much time to contemplate what we should do or how we should do it, we just do it automatically.

Ninety per cent of our total behaviour – experts estimate – is steered by the subconscious! The remaining ten per cent is steered by our psyche, by our logic, by our consciousness.

All of our behaviour is dependent on our imprint. Our behaviour doesn't only entail the things that we do, but also the things that we don't do.

The most obvious difference between a person who's doing really well and another who isn't is about forty centimetres. Forty centimetres is the difference between those who remain sitting throughout life and those who overcome those forty centimetres and get their bottoms off the chair.

How often in life have you said, 'Just once I have to…' or 'One day I'll…' or 'When I find the time I'll…', but you haven't got off your bottom the entire time. This is by no means an accusation, because even this is an automatic behaviour.

We've all learnt that it's better to do nothing. As a rule, this begins very early, at six years old at the latest. When we start school, we learn that we'll be punished for mistakes through bad marks or red marks on our papers. And who wants to be punished? So at some point we reach the decision that it's better to do nothing. This, though, is our biggest mistake.

> I once talked to a priest who administered last rites at a cancer clinic. He spent the entire day speaking to people who would soon die. He told me that he seldom met people who regretted that they had done certain things during their lives. He did, however, meet many people who regretted the things they hadn't done. 'If I'd done this!', 'If I'd done that!', 'If I'd only paid more attention to my health!', 'If I'd only spent more time with my family!', 'If I'd only taken that chance!' If, if, if…!!! But they never got off their bottoms.

Behaviour is likewise *how* I do something. If I take part, if I do what I can, if I keep at it – or if I'm just 'going through the motions'. It's clear that the results here look very different.

Behaviour is also when I do something. There are people who have a special talent for always being a bit late. They consistently hear things like, 'Sorry, but the position's been taken.'

But the way we react to certain situations and people, our choice of words and the way we speak and feel are mostly based on previously learnt and saved processes. Just think about how you speak to small children or with your boss. Without giving it much thought, you choose the appropriate style for each situation.

People think around 60,000 thoughts a day. Do you have any idea what you think about all day and what per cent are thoughts that positively support your goals, behaviour and charisma, and what per cent of your thoughts hold you back?

For a period of 14 days, set the alarm on your watch to ring every hour and write down what you're thinking at the moment the alarm goes off. Then you'll have a pretty good idea how you are programmed day in and day out and the state of your current automatisms!

Another thing on the point of automatism: our brain processes 400 billion bits of information per second, of which we're only aware of 2000 bits. That means that our brain receives 200 million times more data than we're aware of. This alone gives us clear proof of the strength of the power centre that is the subconscious.

When we have these facts in front of us, it becomes clear why new actions only bring specific results when they don't produce new thought models or project something new. Speak to ten people while projecting with at least 90 per cent subconscious communication: 'Nobody speak to me!' There will be little success; a situation that won't improve even if you were to talk to 100 people. If you change your subconscious communication (the inner model) and then speak to ten people with this new model: 'With my good mood, everyone will be happy when I speak to them…', your success rate will rapidly increase.

I often hear scared voices saying, 'Oh my, oh my, that's going to be difficult. Will my subconscious be able to rid itself of the old models of my childhood? After all, I was permanently in the alpha phase then, and now I have to actively try to reach this state.' (More on this later.)

An example that all parents and grandparents know, and even you know, is of how amazing our subconscious is even as adults when it comes to completely overwriting old inner pictures and thoughts. I (Barbel) have three-year-old twins. We're often visited by parents with infants and we know, of course, that our own kids were once that small. But we just can't imagine it any more! This is something that you're always hearing parents say: 'Funny, I can't imagine that my kids were ever that small…'

It isn't really funny at all. You look at your child today with strong emotions and your subconscious saves this most up-to-date picture of your child. 'The old picture's outdated and in the past. We don't need it any more,' says your subconscious and erases the picture from the hard drive.

No matter how old you are, you've only got to convince your subconscious that something is 'old, outdated and not needed anymore'. If you offer it something new, it will overwrite the old and then it's gone.

So at least check a few of your 60,000 daily thoughts for things you can polish up your daily subconscious automatisms with. And then decide anew what you want to think!

Reprogramme behaviour automatisms

Dr Mansukh Patel in his book, *Mastering the Laws of Relationships*, suggests a technique with which a person can do more to change their outlook in three months than through five years' deliberate effort.

You need a candle and ten minutes before going to bed. Sit quietly and look calmly into the candle and allow your thoughts from that day to play before your inner eye like a film. All the while thank yourself for everything that you've done, no matter how you feel about it. If there's something you wish you'd done differently, rewrite this scene of the film in your head and let it play once again.

The trick is that the subconscious right before bed can't differentiate between the new version of the event and the real version. Let's assume that you become angry when a certain button is pushed every day. Then play your film every evening to yourself, in which you turn your attention within yourself in critical situations and concentrate on being relaxed, right in the centre of yourself, with all of your muscles relaxed, and think of how you would like to react if you were free of those unwanted unconscious thought patterns. Even quicker than you can probably imagine, the subconscious accepts these corrections as new automatisms and all of a sudden you can't help but react in any way but the new way. You'd never achieve that as elegantly and smoothly through logic or behaviour training. Because with this technique, your innermost self is thinking that you've always been doing it this way. Try it!

This book offers you a wide variety of possibilities to quickly reprogramme, and if some day that isn't quick enough for you and you want to reactivate the child inside yourself, then you can switch to the international bestseller, *The Cosmic Ordering Service.*

No method is really better or worse than any other, but there is one method that suits you better than any other *now in this moment!* Discovering this is an important first step in discovering the power that is dormant within you.

Let's take a look at body language. Body language is understood as certain behaviour patterns that as a rule cannot be consciously controlled and run automatically in accordance with our inner settings. Besides gestures, intonation, posture and facial expressions, it also includes word choice in the broadest sense, volume while speaking, and the voice and its changes (although this doesn't belong to traditional body language).

Whether we use an especially nice or especially aggressive tone with people during the day, whether we have a cold or warm posture, whether we have a friendly or disagreeable face, depends on our inner settings – our programming. And it's automatically run without us having had a direct influence.

Of course, we can change and adapt these things in relation to our body language, but as soon as we lose absolute control – and who can maintain this over such a long time? – the old automatism will be used again.

The effectiveness of our body language is dependent on whether other people can judge it. Naturally, a trained eye can quickly interpret and react to certain gestures, but even a layman can register these things very well, though subconsciously, and they influence their behaviour.

For this reason, body language is important to us, because we are visual beings. We take in much more information with our eyes than any other sense organ. Pictures, for example, are transported 15 times quicker to the brain than words.

An experiment that I (Clemens) often do in my seminars and workshops is very surprising and impressive to the participants. I ask: 'Please do the following. Raise your arms up *horizontally*.' I, however, raise my arms up *vertically*. Every time I do this experiment the participants raise their arms vertically almost without exception even though I asked them to raise them horizontally. This is a good example of the fact that we react better to things we see than to those that we hear.

An everyday example. When a father tells his child, 'You mustn't lie!' it's an important and sensible piece of information. But when the phone rings and he tells his wife to tell the caller that he's not home, the child won't hear, 'You mustn't lie.' The child will see that Dad is lying. Because the child has seen this example and not just heard the request, they will most likely lie in the future.

If you've got your own kids, you probably also know that there's no logic in teaching them – they'll just copy everything anyway! We as parents should pay attention to setting a good example. We should practise what we preach, as it were. Sure, it's demanding, but it's also the only truly successful method.

Another area in which our physical selves are very much influenced by the programming in our subconscious is our physique. Whether too fat, too thin, too heavy, too light or whether we're a funny shape or well-proportioned is dependent on the model that we've programmed into our subconscious through constant repetition or strong emotion. Of course, our weight is dependent on what and how much we eat. If this was the only thing that was important, then why do we talk of people with a better or worse metabolism? Why do some people crave sweets and others don't? Why do some people stuff themselves until nothing else fits in and others stop eating as soon as they feel full? The answer lies in our programming.

I (Clemens) used to conduct special seminars called 'Think Yourself Thin', which always presented the most bizarre reasons for being overweight. Women whose mothers were fat and whose first and most constant impression of a woman was that of a fat woman. Or many people who were lovingly called 'dumpling' as children. As this pet name is connected with recognition and love, children are keen to comply. And as long as such programming isn't changed, even as adults we will try to remain the 'beloved' dumpling.

Besides other possible causes that begin in childhood, we're also busy embodying such models daily – without wanting to. How many times a day do people with figure problems say, 'I'm too fat!', 'No matter what I eat I put on weight immediately!', 'My clothes keep getting tighter!'? Added to this, of course, is the confirmation we get from those around us. And then we wonder why that's the way it is!

Added to this, such commands as 'Eat everything up' or the conviction that 'Only chubby children are healthy children' follow people through life and drive them so vehemently that responsible, healthy eating behaviours just aren't possible.

Sometimes the causes of obesity can be traced back to specific events.

One woman at such a seminar established that the cause of her plain appearance could be traced back to the following event. As an attractive young woman, she was often chatted up by men, which, because she was a very shy and strictly raised girl, was very uncomfortable for her. The situation escalated when one of these admirers attempted to rape her. This caused the woman, without her consciously realising it, to adopt an unattractive appearance so that no man would ever have such thoughts again. She achieved this goal quite successfully, but at what a price!

Similarly graphic is the example of a man who decided that he needed more space in his relationship. He could hardly even stand being physically close to his wife any more. He felt that everyone was getting too close. And since that time, he subconsciously developed a shield in the form of a belly with a classic 'spare tyre'.

No matter where the causes for being overweight or even underweight or other figure problems come from, a long-term change is only possible when these causes are worked on in the subconscious.

Diets and fasts help, of course, but only as long as you are doing them. The old programme kicks in again quickly, an experience that many of us have had all too often.

The process is clearer when you look much closer at the processes within our bodies. Humans have a whole list of control mechanisms in the body that make sure that certain set values are kept constant; body temperature, for example. It's set at 37°C – or, to be more exact, 36.8°C. We possess a control mechanism that makes sure this temperature is kept constant. If the temperature threatens to decrease, we begin to shiver, which creates warmth. If it threatens to rise, we begin to sweat, which when it evaporates creates coolness against the skin, keeping the temperature constant even here.

A control mechanism works just like a thermostat. Imagine that in the room in which you're sitting there's a thermostat set to 30°C. That's much too warm. If it's cooler than 30°C outside, just open the window and the temperature in the room will go down. When it's cool enough again and you shut the window, it causes the heater to warm up the room to 30°C again. That's its job, after all.

It's just the same when it comes to your figure and weight, the difference being that there are no set values. They're variable. Let's take as an example a man who weighs 100 kilos. While standing naked in front of the mirror in the morning, he decides that it's too much and that it's time to diet (window open). He wants to lose weight, so the body is deprived of calories. He'll tire of this eventually; either because he's lost enough weight or because he just wants to eat a proper meal again (window shut). And he gains back the weight.

But there's something that's crucial, something that is basically brilliant and, in regard to this topic, something rather dramatic!

The heating thermostat that I've just described is really just a stupid machine that does nothing more than calculate: is it 30°C? No. Switch on. Is it 30°C? Yes. Switch off.

Our body, however, is very intelligent. It immediately begins to 'worry' when we diet. It immediately notices that something isn't right. With its instinctual, pre-programmed knowledge, it assumes that there's a crisis; perhaps a famine and the poor person's got nothing to eat. Thank God for the body's stored reserves that it now accesses. As soon as the suspected emergency is over, though, and our guy's eating normally again, the body will refill its reserves.

But there is something crucial to be added here: Let's say the body sets its base weight at 100 kilos. Because the decrease in food caused the body to go below this base, it will think about what it can do to maintain this base weight in the future and what it should do to prepare for another crisis in the future. It will add more to the reserves than it previously had; let's say 105 kilos.

'Obesity through dieting' is an experience that most people who've gone on diets have had. They weigh more after the diet than they did before it.

Statistically, 90 per cent of all people who go on diets weigh two kilos more a year after the diet began than they did before. It can only work in the long term if we change our 'thermostats': that is, if we change the programming of our subconscious.

Another aspect of our physical body that is caused by the programming in our subconscious is our appearance. Do we look young and dynamic, or old and used-up? This has, as you already know, nothing to do with the number of years you've lived, but with these inner settings.

You're only as old (or as young)
as you feel!

Why is it that at class reunions there's always such a difference in apparent age between people who are actually the same age? Just the change in appearance following a hard stroke of fate is proof enough of the influence of the psyche on our appearance. We look so much better when we've just fallen in love than when our relationship has hit a hard patch!

You probably know this effect from a dubious party prank.

A few guests choose a victim at random from the guests at a party and play the following prank on him: the first prankster approaches the guest and asks him if he's feeling ill. After the victim vehemently denies this, the second prankster approaches the victim a few minutes later and also asks if he's feeling ill. By the third or fourth time the victim is approached, he'll begin to feel very ill indeed.

The power of thought!

The relationship between programming and appearance is so striking that it has is own field of science, 'physiognomic psychology'. It is based on the idea that you can tell the character of a person from their appearance, their build, the shape of their face or of their nose, for example. What is character but the programming of our subconscious?

The matter of personal hygiene is also controlled by the subconscious. A woman who is of the opinion that she's unattractive, for example, would never have the idea to do something nice for her appearance. Why should she go to the hairdresser, the beautician? Why should she buy beautiful clothes? In her own opinion, these won't change her unattractiveness. That's just the dog chasing its tail, though! Of course those who do nothing for themselves will look unattractive.

From the body's appearance, it's not such a long jump to the topic of health. Thirty years ago, traditional medicine attributed 20 per cent of all illnesses to psychological causes. Today that figure is 80 per cent. There are in fact doctors today who claim that 100 per cent of all illnesses are psychologically caused. We needn't go that far, though. Even if only 80 per cent of all illnesses are psychosomatic, that means that 80 per cent can be healed through the psyche as well. Traditional medicine doesn't want to look at any of that, though; not that they don't know it. Our health systems don't support these things. For example, if you go to the doctor with stomach problems or even an ulcer, he has to ask if you're having any problems in your life. These conversations don't pay enough, though, for the doctor to pay the rent or the receptionist. The only thing that sustains him and which he has been taught, is prescriptions and surgical treatment.

Problems arise with this attitude, however, whenever 'very clear causes' that are responsible for an illness appear. What's important here is to tell the difference between causes and triggers. The trigger for flu, of course, is the virus a person catches. It isn't the cause, however; that's found one level lower. If the virus were the cause, then everyone who carries the virus would be ill. But why does the immune system work in such a way that the illness doesn't become active in some people, but does in others? The answer is again to be found in the psyche.

There are two aspects to the topic of health. The first is the enormous influence of the psyche on our body, such as in the party example. A lot of people expect to become ill, that they'll get a really bad cold once a year, for example, and so the body reacts accordingly. Placebos are a good example of this. Placebos are medicines that in fact aren't medicine at all. During drug trials on people who have the same illness, one group takes a real medication and another a placebo. Many who simply believe they've received the real medicine become healthier; even those who've received the placebo.

The second aspect is that an illness is a bit like a form of body language. The body wants to say something with it.

If you have a runny nose, for example, you should ask yourself why it is runny. Whom are you 'allergic' to, whom or what can't you bear to see or listen to any more, what is your gut feeling etc.; these things are the real reason for the body's symptoms.

And as long as only the symptoms are treated, without looking at the background causes, you will inevitably experience further, perhaps even worse, symptoms. Even with this, the body is just the mirror of the soul. The tragic thing is the fact that anchored automatisms are always stronger than consciously controlled behaviour. In the end, we will always behave according to our programming and not our own free will.

Our only chance is
to change our programming.

Let's sum all of this up. Everything that occurs often enough and/or causes us very emotionally to consciously think, do, say and feel something is anchored in the subconscious as an automatism, and it will:

- influence our behaviour, as well as ...
- control our physical being in terms of our:
  - body language
  - appearance
  - physique, and even our ...
  - health.

I also like to compare the relationship between the conscious and the subconscious with the idea of a big steamer ship:

> The captain (us and our mind, the conscious) stands on the bridge. This captain sends orders down to the engine-room (to the subconscious). The crew in the belly of the ship carries out these orders. If the same orders are continually given for similar situations, the crew notices this and deals with the situations independently. Now the captain's got his mind free to deal with more important things.
>
> Just like the crew in the belly of the ship can't see where the ship is headed, and pretty much blindly listens, so does our subconscious allow itself to be programmed by our behaviour, no matter whether it's good or bad for us. An order is an order.

Another graphic comparison is with a computer:

> First of all, there are the so-called operating systems and programmes in order to get the whole thing up and running. These operating systems are a set part of any elec-

tronic data programming and are built in at the factory. These represent the base needs as the foundation of the subconscious.

The rest of the hard drive is filled with programmes and data. Data are individual pieces of information that are used as needed. Our subconscious also saves everything that we've done, said or experienced.

The programmes that make it all interesting are our automatisms. The programmer who has entered our programme is ourselves; we with our conscious perception, our conscious thoughts.

If a programme spits out 'rubbish', the reason is, provided the hardware (the body) is functioning properly, that it's been programmed with 'rubbish'.

Combined efficiency of the subconscious and thoughts

Autogenic training wonderfully demonstrates how much anyone can learn to influence systems in their body, which don't actually allow themselves to be influenced through thought. Perhaps you already know some of the typical autogenic training suggestions. The subject lies relaxed on a mat and allows their breathing to slow. Then they begin repeating the following thoughts in their mind: 'My right leg is very heavy. My right leg is getting heavier and heavier…'

You don't have to do this too long before the right legs feels considerably heavier than the left. The same thing happens with our thoughts: 'My left hand is very warm. My left hand is getting warmer and warmer, almost hot.'

Practising two or three times a week, twice a day, almost any-one can get their body to make the desired hand (or foot or what-ever) distinctly warmer than the rest of the body.

How? Isn't body temperature controlled subconsciously and kept constant, in a healthy body at least? But look at how when I know that I want my right hand to be warmer than the rest of my body my body gives in, ignores all of the automatisms and does what I want!

This is good news for us: I'm not dependent on my collected automatisms. No one is forcing me to keep hold of them until the end of my days. The power of my thoughts can bring about new automatisms in my subconscious in many areas.

I can change the programme!

The warmth and heaviness that autogenic training creates are only to switch off and relax. I (Barbel) have met a real sniper. Originally, it made sense if snipers could lower their total body temperature by a few degrees. They could then hide in trenches and become invisible to an enemy that was using heat-sensing devices to detect people. This is no longer an issue as it's long been techno-logically easy to detect the smallest variation in temperature in any environment. The technology is sensitive enough that during fires the source of the fire can be traced, because it always differentiates itself from the rest of the fire through a small difference in temper-ature.

At that time, however, you were the star of the troop if you could lower your body temperature more than anyone else. This is possible through mere exercise in thought concentration. The best results are achieved by those who can best concentrate while simultaneously finding inner relaxation. This isn't done any more as no one can manage to drop their body temperature by 10°C or more and survive.

That ex-sniper was funny. He told me that you have to – much like while playing golf – empty yourself inside and only have thoughts which deal with the goal at hand. How you hold the weapon or how, when, why to flex a muscle or to shoot, are insignificant.

If the mind is clear enough, the body takes control of everything, allowing you to hit the target exactly. Great, isn't it?

When I raise my hand to get a pen, I'm not conscious of how much thought is required to make the muscle move. I don't see anything special about that. But when a sniper is always able to hit his target, even at long distances, and tells me that he empties himself inside and concentrates his thoughts on the precision of his movements, it's like magic to me.

But it's the same type of magic that my thoughts use to create illness or health in my body. If you are interested in a more detailed look at the topic of health, the results of current gene research show that a maximum of two to three per cent of all illnesses are based on gene defects and the rest arise from our own inner settings for life. You can find out more about this in the book *Das Gedächtnis des Körpers* by J. Bauer, a professor of psychoneuroimmunology.

Let's take drawings as another example. Are you a bad drawer? Great, because the next experiment is perfect for you. Try to draw an offended gnome, a stuck-up gnome and a dumb gnome. (I haven't got a preference for negative facial expressions; I just arbitrarily chose these, because I think they're rather hard to draw.)

If you can't draw well, you'll have no idea at first how you should draw an offended face. Except when, and this is the thing, you bring up the feeling of being offended first in yourself. Be absolutely offended about anything. Be angry about whatever it is and let the pen you're using also be offended as you sketch, scratch, scrawl or whatever the gnome's face on the paper. You'll see that, all of a sudden, your lines develop a certain offended movement. That's the secret of a good cartoonist. You feel like the character you want to draw and then the right expression appears automatically. You hand your pencil over to the power of your thoughts (just like the sniper and his weapon and his muscles that he hands over to controlled, precise thoughts) and it takes care of the task for you without you having to work out a plan of how an offended gnome looks.

It's the same with music. If you play an instrument or enjoy listening to live pianists or classical concerts, you've also surely noticed that they can attempt to reproduce moods (with melancholy pieces like 'The Moldau' by Bedřich Smetana, for example) when they play slower, use lighter finger movements and pay strict attention to the rhythm provided in the score. It doesn't sound very happy, that's true, but if you listen closely, you'll hear that it's somewhat mechanical. The emotion doesn't really come across.

If a concert musician loses himself in the music, though, and somehow totally identifies with the melancholy of the music, then all of a sudden they are 'The Moldau'. They don't care what the sheet music says about the tempo and such. They are melancholy personified and anyone can hear this. The entire audience sighs and the use of tissues rapidly increases.

Whoever plays the same piece without the use of the power of thought, whoever loses themselves in neither thought or emotion, will look out onto a yawning audience.

But what does all of that have to do with my life?

You want to be professionally successful, but you're playing the keys of your professional success like the inept pianist. What do you think life is going to do? Exactly. It's going to yawn.

You want to be successful and all of your thoughts and the resulting feelings are fulfilled by this inner picture. It gushes out of your pores, you can sense it in your aura. It's already smiling on your face and from all of your movements. What do you think life will do? After thundering applause, it'll deliver whatever goal you've set for yourself. That's logical; it can't do any differently. Just like a listener who's moved can't do anything but reach for a tissue, life can't do anything but reach for your goals and hand them to you.

You yourself have moved life and the listeners respectively, because this and this living power in yourself were felt and couldn't be resisted!

Relationship example: If you believe that you'll never ever be able to draw an offended gnome, these thoughts will cramp your fingers and your gnome will look as if it has asthma.

If you think, consciously or subconsciously, that you'll never find a partner, because you're not worthy of love, then these thoughts will cramp your very being and your entire appearance will look as though you really aren't worthy of love. This is impossible, though, because everyone's deepest, most natural essence is worthy of love. Have you ever seen an evil baby?

You think: 'Hey, great, that's the way it works. If I imagine myself to be really offended, I'll be able to somehow – presto! – have a gnome with an offended look on his face when I draw him.' Then the gnome will look like this.

Are you one of those people who are under the assumption that everyone likes you, so you won't have to wait very long after a relationship fails until the next person comes along who worships you? Then you've always known that you'll never be alone for long when everyone likes you. So the fact that you're totally boring and our example person above can be a supermodel doesn't play a role.

You can also behave a lot worse than the supermodel. If you think of yourself as worthy of love and the supermodel doesn't, then the supermodel will have no chance against you. That's the reality of the situation and you'd know it if you'd only stop for a moment and think about what the connection between relationships and loving oneself looks like among all of your relatives, friends and colleagues.

They accomplish all of it with their thoughts and subconscious automatisms; the music piece, the gnome face or their body language fit exactly to their thoughts and models. That and nothing else is what you'll project, that and nothing else will be received by others. As surely as every layman can hear if a pianist plays with or without emotion, so certain is it conveyed to another person the feeling that you're worthy of love (or think that you are) or not.

In the end, what shapes your life more? Mere action (playing the piano, drawing, work or relationship) or your thoughts and subconscious automatisms in the particular matter?

The shared subconscious

It's of interest to us now to look at this pattern of the conscious and the subconscious in connection to other people. And there's something really fascinating here.

An interface exists between individual 'subconsciousnesses'. Each person isn't a closed system unto themselves. Information is, subconsciously, without us consciously knowing, passed on. This interface is the basis for specific things such as thought-transference, intuition and love. How else can 'love at first sight' be explained, if not through a multitude of subconscious information?

Proof of the existence of this interface has already been shown in many scientific areas, especially in the field of biology by noted scientist Rupert Sheldrake. He calls these connections the 'morphogenic field' and has even developed a theory for the process of transference. According to him, 'These fields arise through a sufficiently large number of patterns that are rediscovered only through morphic resonance that is based on a kind of rebirth.' (Sheldrake, *The Rebirth of Nature*)

The famous example of the monkey provides an explanation:

Researchers fed potatoes to monkeys on an island. The treats were thrown onto the sand and weren't very tasty with their sandy coating, so individual monkeys began washing the potatoes. Very quickly other monkeys began copying this behaviour. Where at first it was just a few monkeys doing this, this behaviour suddenly began appearing in all monkeys. What was really astounding, however, wasn't just that the monkeys on the one island were doing this, but that even monkeys living thousands of kilometres away copied this behaviour.

(It was, by the way, the Japanese macaque that discovered potato washing in Japan in 1953.)

The biology relates to the principle of the 'hundredth monkey', to which this morphic resonance applies.

Less known and just as impressive is a similar example with rats. The healer Clif Sanderson told me (Barbel) about an experiment that was done in Boston in the '60s:

In the experiment, a rat had to look for a piece of cheese in a maze. Naturally, it often got lost until it was finally able to reach the cheese very quickly and in the most direct way.

When a new rat was put in the maze, it took a quite a while until it found the right path. All of a sudden every rat of the same rat family, even on its first time in the maze, could do this.

And not much later rats worldwide could find the cheese straight off when put into a maze with the same pattern. Even newborn rats came into the world knowing how to find the cheese in the maze straightaway.

A quick question for you: who do you think have the greater potential to summon information from shared fields of subconscious? Rats or people?

Meanwhile, in often very similar experiments, the existence of this interface between other types of animals, between people and even between people and animals has been proven without a doubt. Information that is placed in the subconscious from one or more 'consciousnesses' could be retrieved by any of the individuals involved.

> An example of this between people is clearly shown at the international patent office in Munich. It's very often the case that within a short period of time the same patents are received from different corners of the globe fully independently of each other and without any connection. As soon as an idea is born, it is retrievable by everyone else.

If we remember what we said about our 'one person model', that all things that we've ever felt and experienced are saved in our subconscious, it makes my head spin a bit thinking about this interface.

> *Everything that's ever been thought by a person,*
> *and this includes every action, remark, experience etc.,*
> *is retrievable by every other person*
> *through our shared subconscious.*

Where else would people get information to be able to tell a stranger about their past? People who've got an extraordinarily good access to this 'pot' are called clairvoyants or fortune-tellers. Even when many of these, in my opinion (Clemens, but Barbel agrees), run scams, this doesn't change the good work of really good, genuine fortune-tellers.

I (Barbel) have personally experienced and met many of them. I've described in detail a few of them in my other books, among them Joseph McMoneagle who, with his type of clairvoyance (remote viewing), tracked down abducted soldiers and missing children as well as hidden weapons and mines left over from wars, and even proved this publicly on television shows (on which he found three out of five missing persons). He was in the service of the Pentagon with this ability for 25 years and has now been retired for many years. I was lucky enough to speak to him twice.

As far as clairvoyance goes, a good example is the ever-increasing number of clairvoyant children born over the last few years. The film *Indigo* by Stephen Simons (www.indigo-movie.com) is about a crime that is solved by a super-clairvoyant child. The whole film seems like a fairy story, but such children do exist and the film presents an idea of what their lives are like (for books on the subject, see the list of references). Just such a teenage girl (in reality, not on film!) has tried to network all of the clairvoyant children worldwide, so that she no longer feels alone. She says it's horrible when you can read everyone's thoughts around you. As she's very pretty, many young men around her think sexual thoughts. The poor lads naturally have no idea in how much detail the young woman can understand what they are thinking.

Clairvoyant children or youths automatically instigate a strong kind of mental hygiene, which they immediately put into practice when the person opposite is shocked by a thought that they are having.

But this phenomenon is taken too far in many parts of society. Parents of children who are nothing more than spoiled interpret their strange behaviour as signs of special spiritual ability when all the parents really need is a course in raising their children (above all, a course in raising themselves). This naturally creates the impression for critics that clairvoyants absolutely do not exist. No wonder.

There are life coaches who can help us to discover what our subconscious is thinking, what we are subconsciously telling ourselves. Namely, that often we just lie to ourselves and believe our own fairy stories too much. Luckily, there are various technologies (back speaking, applied kinesiology, RAC, energy field detectors, lie detectors, systematic experiments) to help us research what our thoughts are saying. Some people go to consultants in these fields in order to uncover and resolve their subconscious automatisms and deepest beliefs.

You just can't imagine everything that's out there if you've never looked for it.

But as crazy as it sounds to newcomers or the mildly curious, isn't it great that there are obviously so many people who have a real need to tidy up the old drawers of the subconscious in order to lead a free, authentic and self-realised life?

And in almost all of these methods our own conscious grasps the shared subconscious and 'extracts' the appropriate information. The key element here is the right 'ladle'. (As we said, there's more to it than the layman knows.)

This information doesn't only work between people who are living. We've also received information from our parents: in one form as genes, but also through the shared subconscious. Think about how confidently our children deal with today's technology.

It's not necessary for them to learn it anew. They already 'know' the existence of these things and just use them.

So we get information from our parents, and so the series of information conveyors doesn't end. Because our parents also tapped into their parents and they theirs and so on and so forth.

Basically, all information since humans began thinking is contained in the shared subconscious, an inexhaustible font that we've just got to take advantage of. And whatever we call this source, whether shared subconscious or morphogenetic field, cosmic intelligence or nature, it doesn't matter.

There are people who call this source 'God'. And this inner creative power is also meant by the term 'God'. (The old man with the raised finger on a cloud is just a picture created by the Church.)

Everything that you imagined 'God' to be is within yourself and you have access to it. You are the authority in your life. You shape your life through your thoughts with genuinely 'godly' power.

Get this straight:
you are the creator of your own world.

The shared subconscious

This interface doesn't only function between members of individual species, such as just between humans or just between dogs. In fact, this interface connects everything that exists on earth and even in the entire universe. Just because we don't know about it doesn't change the facts. We actually make subconscious contact with representatives of other species.

What else would you call it when someone who at his dog's smallest whimper knows exactly what the animal wants? Or the other way around: have you ever noticed that dogs can tell if their owner is getting up to take them for a walk or is merely going to the fridge for a beer? Or maybe you know people whom all dogs react badly to or others whom cats trustfully approach? This is where simple models from the subconscious of the person in question are received by the animals. The first person probably had a bad experience with a dog and this programming is set while the other person just loves cats and they notice this.

Every rider can confirm to you that experienced horse people use the reins and whip less often, and that emotional connection plays a much greater role.

We can even communicate with plants through this shared subconscious. You often read about amazing horticultural cultivation in the newspaper. If you ask the gardener for his secret, you often hear that he 'just talked to the plants' and that he 'loves' them. (Naturally, without the use of any questionable chemicals and methods! Who wants to shower something they love with radioactive materials?!)

Speaking of human–plant behaviour, in the last few years and even in the last decades, amazing discoveries have been made in science.

A classic example:
With the help of electrodes from a polygraph machine (lie detector) that were attached to the leaves of a dracaena, a certain Cleve Backster, America's leading lie detector

expert, noticed in 1966 that the plant reacted to his thoughts. He only had to consider singeing one of the plant's leaves with a match and the needle jumped. If he approached the plant with a lit match, without meaning to do anything to it, the plant went 'cold'.

An enormous number of further experiments were and are to this day being done which all come to the same result: plants are able to sub-consciously receive information from us humans, better than we are, even. This connection also exists between animals and plants.

In this way, a philodendron connected to a recording device showed panic when a live lobster in the next room was thrown into boiling water.

Obviously, we humans are a bit behind in this ability. We concentrate on our five senses and forget that in reality there are so many more.

Practise this 'nonverbal communication' a bit for yourself by making intellectual contact with animals or just conversing with an old tree. You'll see after some initial inhibition that it's fun and after some time you can have a real 'conversation'.

Give it a try!

The time when you'd be burnt at the stake for such an activity is, thank God, long past. If a plant knows when a lobster in the next room is being boiled, it just isn't possible that *you*, the crowning achievement of creation, are missing the ability for such percep-tion. Let's be clear about it: this perception *must* exist. It's just buried. Just like a muscle that you put in a cast or don't use for some time falls asleep, in the same way this perception has to be totally trained again when it's been asleep for generations. But I (Barbel) refuse to believe that plants are basically cleverer than people when it comes to this type of communication.

The mechanism of the shared subconscious

Information transfer

As a reminder: we've said that thoughts that occur often enough and/or with intense feeling lead to an automatism in the subconscious and that this programming influences our behaviour.

Thoughts are a form of energy. And just like other forms of energy, our thoughts can be graphically displayed. We use the shape of waves to show this. Each thought is represented by a certain wave pattern. So every thought pattern that is recorded in our subconscious has a very specific wave pattern. And we send, through the interface, this wave pattern to everyone else.

When we meet people whom we find nice straight off, it's because the programming in our subconscious meets another's programming that's identical to ours. We even have a phrase for it: 'We're on the same wavelength.' And this empathy is immediately sensed, even when we only realise after a few hours or days how many beliefs, tendencies, interests and even programmings are the same. If many of the programmes are the same, we call it friendship.

And then it always happens, that for whatever reason someone changes. All of a sudden they're programmed differently. Then the wavelengths don't fit any more, of course, and the love is gone.

This interface, this shared subconscious, has different effects on our lives. The first is the above-mentioned 'information transfer'. That means the programmes in our subconscious influence not only the points in the model for one person, but they are also transferred to everyone else.

Example: imagine that you want to apply for a new job and already have an appointment for an interview. You've learnt about the conscious and the subconscious in the previous section and now know that our behaviour is very important, so now you're attending a course in job interviews where you can learn proper behaviour (they really do exist!). You'll also learn the correct body language there, in order to be non-verbally convincing as well. Besides that, you also look at your appearance, of course. You'll dress appropriately for the future task and perhaps even go to the hairdresser's beforehand. You probably won't be able to do anything about your physique so quickly, but you'll dress so as to appear dynamic. You wouldn't go to an interview with a horrible cold, so you're also best prepared as far as the topic of health goes. All of the points from the model described above are taken care of to the highest level of satisfaction.

And now you're sitting across from your potential boss and you're telling him, from your conscious to his, what a great person you are for this job. This is communication that's 'up above'.

You may have a very old programme from your childhood deep down in your subconscious that says, 'I'll never amount to anything!' Someone close to you probably continuously drummed this negative message into you.

And even this message will be perceived by the person across from you – subconsciously via this interface, 'down below', as it were. Depending on their sensitivity, your potential boss will describe this as a 'feeling', 'intuition' or 'sixth sense'. In any case, they'll allow themselves to be influenced by this feeling and perhaps spontaneously say to you, 'Thanks a lot. We'll be in touch. Don't call us, we'll call you!' And that'll be that.

That means that this subconscious information transfer can make the best studied techniques all for nothing. Everything that's 'up above' is a bit like a puppet show where the actors are visible behind the curtain.

The second point, which is caused by the connection of individual 'subconsciouses', is the so-called 'filtered perception'.

Filtered perception

Think for a moment about how much information streams into us and how much of it we actually register. Apart from the temperature and humidity, the weight of our clothing on our skin, all of the background noise and even more that normally escapes our attention, are the other things that we only notice when they really interest us – with which we often busy ourselves and of which we have an appropriate model in our subconscious.

Everyone knows this or a similar situation: you want to buy a new car and you've decided on a brand and a certain model. And suddenly 'everyone' is driving that car. You're constantly seeing it. There weren't that many of them before! (Of course, there were always that many, but you just never noticed.)

The principle is the same as with the radio or television. There are, let's say, hundreds of stations out there on the ether. There's a radio on the table that's tuned to a specific wavelength. This radio filters this station out from the many other stations. And if you could ask the radio how many stations there were, it would tell you with utter conviction that there was only one.

And in exactly the same way we perceive, based on the wavelength of the model in our subconscious, the things in our environment that correspond to that model. Selective, filtered perception based on our interests and inclinations, our beliefs and ideas.

This is very sensible: what interest are the dogs running round the park to me if I'm a flower lover? I'd notice every flower, but if someone were to ask me how many dogs there were in the park, I wouldn't be able to say.

On the other hand, this selective perception can be problematic. The models in our subconscious aren't always very positive.

If I were someone who was annoyed by the dirty state of the park caused by dog-dirt, then I'd only notice that. I'd know exactly how many dogs were in the park and how many piles they'd left behind that day. And I probably wouldn't notice a single flower except to see that a dog had done its business in a flower patch.

The same principle is true for both cases: we perceive exactly that which corresponds to our wavelengths. In the second case, though, we would hardly have enjoyed the day. Terrible, really, when there were so many flowers out there!

Put a group of people in a row side by side and ask each of them to describe what they see. Even though objectively they should perceive everything the same, you'll get different descriptions without exception.

Perception is dependent on our programming,
and this is individually different.

Basically, there is no objective 'truth', as 'truth' is that which we hold to be 'true'. In our realistic world, we only hold as true that which we can register with our five senses. And even the perception of the sense is, as we've seen, dependent on our inner settings and our expectations, so is really quite subjective.

There's another catch to this filtered perception: we form very exact opinions of things, in that we constantly think the same thoughts. We automate everything in the subconscious. Due to this programming, we have a limited perception and primarily notice the things that correspond to our opinion.

And then we speak, often boastfully, of our 'experiences'. (The motto being: 'You see! I knew it!' But we didn't really foresee it. We really caused it through our programming!)

And these experiences again confirm our conviction that we think the same thoughts again and set the model. It's a vicious circle.

As an example, I'd like to cite Ludwig, a representative of every person who's of the opinion that 'The world's horrible, everything used to be better and everyone wants to box me round the ears.' Because of this setting, he really only filters the negative aspects of his life, strengthened through his programming, behaves accordingly and gets exactly what he expects.

We can only break this vicious circle when, despite our 'experience', we plant thoughts in our subconscious that don't necessarily reflect reality but contain what we'd like to have.

Subconsciously filtered perception

In order to understand the extent of our filtered perception, individual and collective, we want to take to heart a small digression courtesy of elementary particle physicist and winner of the Right Livelihood Award, Professor Hans-Peter Dürr.

Let's look at filtered perception as if we are being confronted by topics like the ones hitherto presented for the first time, and that we've never heard that we, through our thoughts and ideas about the world, through our subconscious automatisms, and through our filtered perception, shape and form our reality. Our automatisms then appear to stand in contrast to the popular scientific opinion. All too often these things give the impression that an objective world exists and that subjective impressions are only to do with psychology and nothing to change the big real reality. In order to free us a bit from stiff ideas about our reality, I'd like to quote here, with the kind permission of the Global Challenges Network,

Professor Dürr from his lecture at the Deutsches Museum from his series 'Science for Everyone' in Munich in 1998:

> Our perception of reality, including scientific perception in its strictest form, is similar to a meat grinder. Reality is shoved in at the top and sausages come out the front. The entire world is made up of sausages. It no longer has anything to do with true reality.

I (Barbel) could laugh about this comment by Professor Dürr for hours. It's such a relief for someone like me who belongs to those people who feel a bit like they've gone through the grinder, in terms of what we generally can believe about our reality, to hear this feeling expressed so clearly.

The astrophysicist Arthur Stanley Eddington makes a similar comparison to the ways of science. He reduces reality down to a type of fish. Only fish that fit into the net of the limited scientific perception are accepted as fish. Every fish that's too small for the net and passes through it is seen as nonexistent. Or, to put it another way, only that which is conservatively researched within the relatively coarse possibilities of science is accepted as real.

Due to this short-sightedness, according to Professor Dürr, religion can never come into conflict with science, because religion is based on a reality that is smaller than the mesh of the net that is science. It is based on something for which scientific research criteria are too primitive and which cannot be understood by them.

Due to the limits of scientific thought, which deals only with large fish that get caught in the net, it doesn't touch on our reality.

Matter is an intangible structure of possibilities left by the wayside, suspended in time. 'In a way, matter is a crust of the mind, a type of crusted mind', to cite Dürr again. Even matter isn't as stable or predictable as we used to think. More than 99 per cent of matter is vacuum. The universe is primarily empty. Particles disappear and reappear in it. There's nothing static there. According to American researchers, the most static thing about matter is the information it contains.

Who's surprised then that visualisation techniques and mind training have become so widespread? They are the subconscious attempt of matter to give new ideas. A good and useful thought, I find.

What does reality look like, then?

A quote from the American film *What the Bleep Do We Know!?* says that 'Anyone who isn't curious about such questions is obviously three-quarters dead already.'

Professor Dürr said shortly, concisely and brilliantly in one of his lectures in 1999 that an electron is actually just a kind of field of expectation, a field of possibilities, nothing more. 'This field of expectation in the future will develop like a wave and then form in a different place as a new electron. I have measured it. Absolutely nothing has moved between the two locations. Rather, the electron has disappeared from one location and reappeared in another.'

Heisenberg had already said in his time that electrons and atoms aren't things, but tendencies. Today many researchers see them as only 'possibilities of the conscious'!

For some this idea is too abstract, because, for one thing, an electron is such a small thing flying somewhere around an atomic nucleus. But the entire material world is made up of nothing more than such atoms. Our entire world is made up of nothing more than fields of expectation that disappear from one location and reappear in another. How is it then that our world isn't in a chaotic state of change if atoms are obviously disappearing every second and are constantly recreating themselves simultaneously?

Professor Dürr says, 'Matter is something that has no new ideas, as it were.' For this reason it is always copying itself. We can perhaps best imagine it with the help of our own thoughts: every time we grasp a concrete thought we commit, according to Dürr, mass murder of the other options we could have thought of. At that moment, all of our possible thoughts solidify into a single one that we actually think.

Professor Dürr occasionally compares reality to a poem. Let's assume that our reality is a poem. If I don't understand the language of the poem, but just add up the same letters and create a list and statistics then this makes enough scientific understanding of the poem to compile technical data from it, like assembling cars and so on. But this is a very limited understanding: there's no true understanding of the poem though this action. Thank you to Professor Dürr for his humorous and valuable work in this field.

If you would like to know about him and his work as well as lecture dates, the information can be found on the Internet at www.gcn.de. GCN is a society that invites global thinking and networked action to secure the sustainability of our planet. GCN, which was founded by Professor Dürr, who is also the chairman of the organisation, can be contacted at:

Global Challenges Network e.V.,
Frohschammerstrasse 14
80807 München,
Tel. +49 (0) 89-3598246

Now let's take a closer look at filtered perception. Filtered perception isn't only related to perception with our five senses. Seeing as how the information is in large part exchanged subconsciously, naturally this selectivity is found here as well. When we spontaneously decide on one partner out of a large number of potential partners, for example, it's always because the programming of that person is identical to our beliefs for a possible partner. Whether they're positive or negative doesn't play a role.

> For example, you as a woman have the task of picking out a man from a group which is totally unknown to you. You can be sure that you'll choose exactly the man who embodies your idea of 'the man'. If you're of the opinion perhaps that men don't do anything around the house, then you'll find one who doesn't. Even if among all the men to choose from there's only a single one!

We always choose people who have the same wavelengths as us. Just like with the radio.

> Or the example of the woman who had four different partners who all hit her. Not that she wanted it, no, just the opposite. And the men's tendencies only came to light after a few days. There weren't, outwardly, any similarities between the men. Until the woman, who now saw the psychic foundations, noticed that the reason had to lie within her. And she remembered that her father used to beat her mother. This experience anchored itself so solidly as a pro-

gramme in the little girl that it became normal to her for women to be physically beaten by men. And in the choice of her partners, she always, subconsciously of course, chose men who corresponded to this programming.

More familiar examples:

A lot of people who are of so-called advanced age and looking for a partner (again), are convinced that 'at their age' every possible partner is either married or that 'something' isn't quite right with them (otherwise they'd be married!).

This conviction always leads the person to meeting potential partners who really are married or who really do have something wrong with them.

They don't notice anyone else due to their filtered perception. They don't correspond to their wavelengths.

You certainly know the situation when you, seemingly contrary to all common sense, have a certain feeling. You're sitting across from someone who, you consciously observe, must be very nice. But somehow you've got a funny feeling in your gut. Now you're receiving subconscious information that doesn't agree with your wavelengths. There's disharmony.

You feel what's really happening in this person no matter what they say to you. And you've got a better chance to react to this person.

This integrated information transfer, consciously through the five senses and subconsciously through feeling, is naturally much more clairvoyant than the first way. We all use this second way daily, only we're usually not conscious of it and even when we notice it we often mistrust it. What's more, it's much more valuable than our logic.

Filtered perception from the outside to us

Naturally, this filtered perception doesn't only work for information that we receive, but also the other way round. Just as we perceive our surroundings after our convictions, naturally so does everyone else.

> Let's put the woman from the earlier example with the men who hit her, alone in a café. The first man who speaks to her is likely a potential beater. It makes absolutely no difference from which direction it comes. Whether he finds her likeable or she finds him likeable doesn't matter. The wavelengths are the same.

And so we have the same effect, due to our inner model, on others. It's not enough that we make our programming, our convictions, known through our behaviour, our clothes, personal hygiene, manner, speech, gestures, intonation etc. – all things that we can perceive with our five senses.

Even when we can sell ourselves so well outwardly, the subconscious information will always be well received by our surroundings. The others will feel it whether it's conscious or not. And they will allow themselves to be influenced by this feeling, whether they're conscious of it or not. There are, of course, enough examples of unscrupulous cheats who project seriousness and find enough customers without their feeling it.

There are two simple reasons, however. One reason is that we in our Western industrial society are very 'headstrong', meaning that we've forgotten to listen to our feelings and instead decide everything very logically. It's just that logical arguments have always had enough intelligent cheats at hand.

There's another reason: many people are convinced that our society today is teeming with cheats. Everyone just wants to get their hands on your money without offering anything in return. When our crook comes into contact with a person with such beliefs, they will have a 'good' feeling about it. What comes across subconsciously from the crook corresponds to exactly what the victim has saved in their subconscious.

The fact that the victim no longer has any good feeling after discovering the crime has nothing to do with it.

What's important is the synchronicity of the programmes that draw on each other.

Any crime, to stick to the same example, is made up of at least two people: the victim and the culprit. The victim sends their belief in the form of very exact wavelengths 'into the ether' – concretely into the shared subconscious. The culprit, for their part, looking for a possible victim, searches the ether for wavelengths that suit their own, without even being aware of this process. And they'll find exactly those people who correspond to their criminal wavelengths.

I don't want to say, of course, that every victim is a criminal. But every victim has, somewhere in their subconscious, a set programme that immediately connects to this. This can, for example, create a huge fear that sooner or later the people they fear will be pulled towards them as if magnetically. Just like the woman who fears violent men and then magnetically draws them to her.

Furthermore, such programming could, for example, be read as: 'The world's a bad place and full of crooks' or 'I'm scared of being mugged' or 'It's been happening so much recently' etc., etc., etc.

Do you remember all the headlines about dog attacks? At some point, a dog attacked someone and the press made a big to-do out of it, resulting in a whole series of incidents involving attack dogs. And why? Because people used the collective power of their fear to bring it about.

That doesn't mean the warnings and reports are bad or condemnable. But when the warnings and reports stir up fear, the exact opposite is achieved, namely more of what was supposed to be avoided! The same system naturally, to get to a happy topic, also works for positive behaviour between business partners, sellers–clients or between man and wife.

Let's say you're looking for a new business partner. The first thing you've got to do is give your subconscious the required information. If you aren't quite sure what qualities your new associate should have and you haven't anchored this model into your subconscious, you'll either never find a partner or find one that corresponds to your old models. If you don't know whether or not such a model already exists or what it looks like, you'll find out as soon as the new man or woman is standing before you.

So please don't complain if you don't like the person. They completely correspond to your inner programming.

Let's summarise. Everything that we do often enough and/or think, do, say or perceive with very strong emotion will be saved in our subconscious as an automatism. This model leads to us

1. being led in our corresponding behaviour
2. being led in our physicality in terms of body language, appearance, physique and health
3. transferring our subconscious information (whether we want to or not)
4. using filtered perception to sense our surroundings according to our models (through our five senses, but also subconsciously)
5. being perceived by our surroundings according to our models (also through the five senses and subconsciously).

Everything that happens (or doesn't happen), how we feel, the way we live and work, has to do with the kind of thoughts we have. If you accept this fact unconditionally, you have every possibility in life.

We are very quick to assume responsibility for positive events. We're always the cause of success. Negative things are usually blamed on others. We always find ways in which others and external factors have caused us to fail.

Only when you really say 'yes' to everything in your life, when you truly accept all responsibility for what happens in your life, do you have the chance to change, without external influences, everything in your life.

You have the power!

Other people reflect
our own inner convictions
back to us.
Even our situation in life
is a mirror
of our subconscious programming.

So, if you want
to change the world,
you have to change yourself!

☆ ☆ ☆ ☆

☆ The Mirror ☆

If it's the case that we only ever perceive what's available in our subconscious as a model, then the people and situations in our surroundings also act as a mirror for us.

And actually, as unbelievable as it perhaps sounds, our surroundings simply mirror our inner convictions. To make this a bit clearer, we'll divide all of the possible mirrors into two basic categories: people and situations. We'll start with people: everything that we especially notice about other people, whether positive or negative, always has in fact something to do with us and our inner programming.

As we generally tend to overlook positive characteristics in others or rate their bearers as 'nice', we'll focus on the negative habits of our dear fellow humans. This is where we find, as so often in life, our big chance to learn. Fundamentally, there are four different mirror aspects:

1. Our own behaviour

Everything that we don't like about the person opposite us, we don't like because we basically behave in the same way. We just don't notice. This is natural, and especially as the first point really quite amazing. I admit it! (As reassurance: there are three more points coming up that are less scary and perfectly suited as a 'lifeline'.) But this first point makes up the biggest part of the mirror.

Let's remind ourselves of filtered perception: we can really only see what we have as a model inside.

Every time a horrid person is standing in front of you and is really getting on your nerves, check to see if others notice this same behaviour in them.

We're absolutely great at seeing ourselves having the wrong impression of ourselves. (All the better that enough mirrors are running around in this world!)

I'll admit that this point, provided that it is really correctly analysed, can be really painful. And very often our ego defends itself powerfully – 'Me? Really? No!'

Unfortunately, this often leads to throwing out the baby with the bathwater, that is to say our wanting to give up on real personal development, because we don't want to understand a certain situation as a mirror.

'There's no way I can be like him. Forget the whole thing!'

I suggest observing this first point in a third party, as much as possible in people that we have a more neutral feeling for.

The next time you're telling a colleague how badly your boss acted again, check to see if your colleague sees the situation exactly as you do.

You'll be surprised to see how often this first mirror point, our own behaviour, is really correct. And when you then, gradually, understand the accuracy of this theory in others, you'll increasingly recognise this in yourself as well.

So notice how you sometimes behave just like the other person (perhaps just 'yourself' on the other side of the table), so thank yourself very kindly on the inside that they're nice enough to help you in a pinch. And in future, try to change this negative behaviour in yourself.

When you've really given up the corresponding behaviour, you'll notice – oh, wonder of wonders! – that you no longer notice this behaviour in others, or it doesn't bother you any more. The sounding board is practically gone. What else will be reflected when there's nothing more there?

It's common for a sudden change to occur just by recognising the mirror.

2. Desired behaviour

The second possibility is that certain behaviour in others only bothers us because we want to be that way. The mirror exists through our envy. We see that others have or can do something that we want to have or be able to do, and we become annoyed with ourselves. And we project this frustration onto others in that we reject them. By rejecting others for what we actually want, we have a good reason not to have it ourselves. In the end we just reject it.

So we're in the clear. We don't have to make an effort and above all we don't have to take responsibility for the fact that we've failed.

Naturally, this is a naïve miscalculation. As long as we repress our desires, we can never fulfil them. And as long as we haven't fulfilled them, in whatever form (see Maslow's hierarchy of needs), we'll be envious of others.

So in the future please think about when that dandy comes in again with his new designer suit and he races by with a blonde in his new sports car if that bad feeling in your gut isn't just a reflection of your desire for those very things.

And if that is the case, then think about how you can get all of those things. Just ask the dandy. Maybe he'll give you a few pointers.

As soon as you recognise this mirror function, the bad feeling in your gut will change into 'Look, there's someone driving a sports car, just like the one I'm going to have. Great!'

In any case, though, and this is crucial, you won't feel bad in these situations any more.

3. Avoidance behaviour

This is the lifeline for all those who 'will never be like that person and will never want to be'. They want to avoid displaying this exact behaviour at all costs. They never want to be that way.

But how is it then with avoidance?

Ask a non-smoker (which ideally is yourself) if they have to avoid smoking. They'll deny this. I only have to avoid something if I have the tendency to do it. The action has to be set inside, so that it has to be avoided on the outside, and prevented from happening at the last minute.

So here's another tendency in me and this will be reflected. You can see: again it all depends on ourselves! So the lifeline isn't so great after all!

The solution is found in point one, in that the existing behaviours shouldn't be attacked, but rather the inner programming.

4. Memory

This fourth and last point brings us to behaviour research. You may know the story of Pavlov and his dogs:

> Pavlov, a Russian physiologist and winner of a Nobel Prize at the beginning of the twentieth century, studied the salivation reflex in a dog in his lab. With special probes, he could establish that every time he put food down in front of the dog its mouth 'began to water'. Not very interesting yet. Every time he opened the lab door to feed the dog, a bell rang. The dog learnt that there was a direct connection between food and the bell.
>
> This connection became so set in the dog that its mouth began to water when the bell was chimed even when there was no food.

Science calls this a 'reflex action' or 'classical conditioning'.

It is seldom considered that we humans in our daily lives are very often also conditioned to certain triggers. This why the behaviour, voice, gestures or whatever of strangers bother us so, because we connect that same behaviour to totally different people of whom we have negative memories. Basically, we've got nothing against these people who are standing in front of us, but we're remembering someone else.

So no reason to get upset about them. They can't do anything about the fact that they've got the same shaped nose as my uncle who used to horribly thrash me as a child.

There are, however, also the problems that we had at that time with those people which came from one of the first three points. Memory is only a time-delayed form of the mirror.

So in summary we can see that everything we notice about other people doesn't originally have anything to do with these people, but with our programming. They always reflect our subconscious programming, because

- we are that way ourselves, or
- we want to be that way, or
- we never want to be that way (but have the possibility of being so), or
- they remind us of others.

If we keep this reflection function clearly in sight, we'll get on well with everyone. That doesn't mean that we have to be best friends with everyone, but at least we haven't got any negative feelings any more. (And you know how negative feelings lead to negative models!)

So in the future when something bothers you about someone and you want to insult them, just think to yourself: 'What was that with the mirror?'

You don't really mean them, you mean yourself. So you can save yourself the insults. And you can switch over to normal contact.

However, should someone insult you, you can think about the mirror anyway and think to yourself: 'Good that I could act as your mirror. But I know that you don't really mean me, but yourself.' And so even here we can avoid fights and anger.

In the morning when you go into the bathroom and look into the mirror and see a horrible uncombed Thing, who combs you then? You or your reflection?

You see! In the real world, we always want to change our reflection. And that, of course, helps about as much as in the bathroom in the morning.

Many people go through life in ignorance of these things and smash the mirror they're looking into. This smashing is called something else in life. In life it's called: separation, divorce, firing, moving house or whatever things have to do with external change.

The person who separates from their partner without having seen the mirror, will inevitably have the same problems the next time.

You surely know people who always have the same kind of partner, boss, co-worker or neighbour.

Of course! If I smash the bathroom mirror because I don't like the look of the person in it, I'll just wind up seeing the same person again in the next mirror. I don't want to say that you should keep every relationship and every job for ever and ever. A change is only sensible when I've learnt what the others reflect to me. Otherwise I stumble into the same traps. And when I've learnt, when I've changed my programming, my beliefs, often a separation is no longer necessary or happens harmoniously on its own.

So start with yourself. Change your model, your behaviour and the world will change.

If you want to change the world,
you have to change yourself.

As the clear recognition of the mirror now and then requires closer inspection, I (Clemens) would like to relate an experience from my practice:

A seminar participant, Paul, after long contemplating the mirror, turned to me as he was of the opinion that he had a concrete example of where this model didn't really apply.

The situation was this. Paul was a member of a very large family that frequently met for get-togethers. The normally good harmony was ruined by a male member of the family. The man was a smoker and didn't want to not smoke at these get-togethers, even though Paul had just had a child and the baby was affected by the nicotine cloud. Due to this situation there was always a lot of anger and the festivities usually ended in a argument.

Paul asked me, almost angrily, where the mirror was now. First of all, he was a non-smoker; second, he didn't want to smoke; third, he didn't have to avoid it since, as a non-smoker, he had no longing for it; and fourth, he'd never experienced anything like it, so it couldn't be a memory.

The anger didn't meet, as so often, the superficially visible topic, the smoking, but obviously something totally different.

So I asked him what really annoyed him in this whole story. And Paul very quickly realised that it was the thoughtlessness of the man. Without a care for the others, he just did what he wanted.

So we found new grounds for the mirror and went through the individual points.

Was Paul thoughtless? Of course not.

Did he occasionally want to be a bit more thoughtless? And then it clicked in him. Paul was a person who always put his own needs and desires last. He always showed consideration, cared for others, just not for himself.

So I suggested to him that in the future he should put a few more of his own interests in the foreground, to be a bit more self-centred. Naturally it should be done in small steps, but they should be consistent. With this suggestion, we parted.

We met again after a few months and he told me the rest of the story. After he saw that the anger with his relative was actually envy, and he had begun to realise his own desires, he suddenly had a different view regarding the smoker. And through this new view, he could approach him very differently. What had earlier happened as an attack or blaming, now became a normal conversation.

Paul told me how he explained his views to the smoker in gentle words in relation to his small child and how after this open, harmonious conversation the smoker was suddenly prepared to smoke outside in front of the door. He hadn't thought of doing this before, because he was always being attacked.

So you see, the mirror always works, even when we might have to polish it a bit. The reflection function is usable for any type of situation.

Through the filtered perception, it is only those situations which stand out or especially speak to us that correspond to our inner programming. We'll always pick out those events which confirm our beliefs. It's also here that what we perceive as the things around us – which is not identical to that which happens around us – are a mirror for us.

So we push against situations that we don't like at all, so we have to admit to ourselves that it depends on us if and how we perceive these situations.

As a rule, we are quick to assume personal responsibility for positive events.

But what's interesting and important are the things that we don't like. It is mainly in this area that our potential for development lies.

Herein lies the chance to connect our inner programming to the outside world and accordingly to work on the 'within' in order to achieve better results on the 'outer' in the future.

I (Barbel) want to talk about one last thing on the subject of 'the mirror' from the Sufi. Sufism is a mystic wisdom teaching and has its own very interesting perception on the topic of 'the mirror in others'.

The Sufis assume that every person has every divine quality innately inside them. That is, for example: self-esteem, wisdom, ability, power in the positive sense, wealth, beauty, good and so on.

Then a person is born to experience some of these qualities in a very special way for themselves. They do this by first living the opposite. In that if you first live in the 'cold', you experience every instance of warmth with special intensity.

We experience this among others so that we – usually due to a lack of self-esteem – can't imagine how many amazing things are within us. Or put another way, we don't allow ourselves the corresponding qualities, because we believe we aren't allowed to. But we see them (the mirror) immediately in others and we get angry when others allow themselves these qualities that we don't allow ourselves.

Just like Paul the non-smoker, then, who didn't allow himself to put his own needs in the foreground. He drew to himself a response with an encounter with someone in his surroundings that lived this quality richly. Paul had barely 'experienced' these qualities himself (and perhaps less convinced, but harmoniously) and he was able to gracefully solve the problem with the smoker.

Inspiration is therefore when you allow all of the qualities, which you want to be part of your soul, and say to all of them, 'I'm allowed.' Then you won't need a mirror any more and you perceive beauty and perfect expression everywhere.

Triggers and symptoms
Are found on the outside,
in the tangible.

Reasons/causes
Are always found on the inside,
in the mind and soul.

☆ ☆ ☆ ☆

☆ Using problems ☆

Every cloud has a silver lining.
You look for the clouds
Because you need the silver lining.

Richard Bach

Oh, all the problems we've got!

Problems with our boss, with our partner, with the kids, with the neighbours (those weirdoes!), with money, with our health, with our physique or just with ourselves.

I think that if we were to make a list of our problems, we could easily fill a book the size of the New York telephone directory.

On the other hand, were you to list the causes of the problems, you'd get by with a lot less paper. And you know the main cause for all of our problems: our own thoughts!

When we said in the previous chapter that other people and also the situations that we experience are really just a mirror to ourselves, to our inner beliefs, our programmes, then it's also clear that our problems don't represent anything else. And these programmes, as we've seen, are a result of our thoughts.

Problems are external signs that there is still programming in our subconscious that doesn't contain what we consciously desire.

There are then indications that there are still things that can be improved a little. And when we improve them, our conditions in life will improve.

So problems – closely looked at – are something very positive!

They're not called 'pro'-blems and not 'con'-blems for nothing. So 'pro'-blems are 'for' something, not 'against' something, and absolutely not against ourselves. On the contrary, they're for us. They're there so that we can constantly improve, that we learn and that we continue to further develop.

Learning doesn't stop when we leave school, training or university. Many are of the opinion that by thirty, they'll have everything sorted; they'll have their career in order, family and home will be on course, so full steam ahead to retirement!

But life makes sure that even these people don't stop learning. It does this by – and I mean this in a nice way – sending problems their way.

The unfortunate thing about learning is, and we were already aware of this at school, that this learning only works through suffering. Instead of seeing a mistake as an invitation to change something, we're punished with a bad mark.

Imagine how developed science would be, if every mistake were punished. Scientists understand that a mistake shows you how something doesn't work and that you've just got to look for another way.

Thomas Edison made over 10,000 mistakes while developing the light bulb. If he'd given up because of 'such big problems' after a few attempts, as most of us probably would've done, you'd have to read this book at night by candlelight. (Which admittedly can be very romantic, but isn't always.)

Due to this false programming, that mistakes are something bad, we don't trust ourselves at all any more to try something new. You could make a mistake and fail. You could cause problems for yourself.

But, as already mentioned, we never get round to learning. And that is where the second possibility is to learn – besides through suffering – which is voluntary, we can freely decide what things to learn.

And what we should (voluntarily) learn we see in our lives every day. These things reflect our inner model and that contains enough potential for change.

If we accept our lives as mirrors, we can see outside events as signals for us to change ourselves. That's how we learn voluntarily.

If we ignore these signals and see these things as 'pure coincidence' and as things that have 'absolutely nothing to do with me', then these signals will become ever clearer until they reach a point where we see them as problems.

> *Problems are nothing more than neglected,*
> *unrecognised signals for our own change.*

And when the problems become big enough, we are no longer willing to take them on in order to solve them. But we should concentrate on the problems within us first, otherwise they are not solved properly and keep coming back.

Let's take for example a manager whose task it is perhaps to learn to pay more attention to his body, to allow his body more calm. His behaviour is going in quite the other direction. He's of the opinion that you have to give everything for your career, that money and status symbols are the most important thing.

Now he's receiving signals from his environment, as a mirror, naturally, for inner instructions for 'calm'.

The first signal might be a television programme where he notices the immense workload of a politician. How can someone work so hard without getting ill?

The second signal is his neighbour who fell asleep behind the wheel of his car and, caused a – thank God, only minor – accident. The neighbour is closer to home than the politician, but it still doesn't have much to do with the manager.

His wife comes into play for the third signal. She tells him clearly that he works too much and he needs to pay more attention to his health. He doesn't see this as a signal either and ignores it. 'Women are always so anxious.'

The fourth signal is even stronger. A good colleague who's got a similar workload to his gets seriously ill. Diagnosis: too much stress. But 'There are just some people who aren't cut out for the tough world of business.' He doesn't notice this signal either.

It can continue in this way to the point where he himself suffers a heart attack. Now he's got a real problem. This problem doesn't leave him with a choice any more how he should learn his lesson. Now he's in hospital. Now he's got calm. Now he pays attention to his body.

(Unfortunately, there are still people who still don't see these strong signals and then die from their third heart attack 'out of the blue'.)

Had our manager seen early enough that the individual 'coincidental' events were basically the mirror for himself, he could have avoided the really big problems. Had he learnt voluntarily, he could have avoided all the suffering.

Think about your own life for a minute. Pick a big problem and think about which base model, which programme, could be behind it. Which psychological cause could be behind it?

And now go back and think about which things pointed in its direction and happened to you before you had this problem.

I'm sure, if you're open to it, you'll find a whole series of situations that were signals that you quite obviously didn't see as such (otherwise the problem would never have arisen).

What does it want to tell me?

When you open yourself up more and more, you'll learn voluntarily as soon as you perceive or experience extraordinary things. Even when you really have problems, you'll see them as invitations to learn and won't feel like a victim of circumstance any more.

Problems are 'for' something, mainly for the right direction.

Whenever we act against our nature, ignore our real abilities and gifts or act against ourselves, we'll have problems.

But the great thing is: everyone who acts according to their nature, everyone who uses their abilities and gifts, everyone who acts for themselves, leads a successful and happy life.

Problems are hints how we can lead a better life, how we can be more successful and happier. Problems are signposts that show us the right direction.

So don't be against your problems. Don't fight them. Be even a bit thankful occasionally if you have a small problem. It will give you the chance to recognise your role of responsibility and bring you a considerable step closer to more satisfaction and happiness.

Self-worth

Besides the necessity of recognising that problems present a mirror of our thoughts, there's a further support in order to approach problems more easily.

These thoughts come from our upbringing. If a child is given a low sense of self-worth while growing up, because they're constantly told everything they've done wrong or even that they're not worthy of love when they don't behave, and so on, then that child will fear making mistakes later in life!

Then the child has stored the terrible thought models from their childhood: that mistakes prove that they're unlovable; so the child avoids them at all costs. Mistakes can only be avoided when you try absolutely nothing new and when you don't touch on your problems, but just leave everything as it is and put the blame on others. Then they become the ones that are unlovable and you're not taken to task any more.

When someone makes a neutral comment about such a person, then that person automatically perceives the comment as a slight against him and broods frustrated for hours about a totally trivial comment.

What does it look like when a child's given a positive feeling of self-worth on its path to adulthood? If the parents, instead of saying, 'If you do that, I won't love you any more,' had said things like, 'I'll always love you. You're a great kid, but it's not okay when you do this and do that!'

This child isn't usually punished for silly things that they've done. Instead, the parents have made an effort through natural consequences (whoever makes a mess has also got to clean it up and miss a fun activity like playing with friends) in order to cleverly bring the child to think: 'Oh, so when I do this or that, I'm still loved, but it has consequences on my wellbeing. Then maybe I'll just leave it alone in the future. So even when I do super-stupid things, my parents still think I'm a valuable person and they even trust me to fix the problems myself – my parents are my best guides. Hmmm… if my parents believe that, then it has to be true…' Through these thoughts and their repetition, the child saves this thought in their subconscious: 'I'm worthy of love and clever and can solve all of my problems!'

The future adult who's grown up with such a positive sense of self-esteem doesn't take a long time when problems arise: they roll up their sleeves and get to work. So even when they make 10,000 mistakes just like Thomas Edison, they don't have any fear of these mistakes. They don't connect them to their own self-worth and they aren't afraid of them. Such a person doesn't take the comments of others personally. Neither do they constantly block communication with others.

So we can see that we can solve every problem much more easily if we have a positive sense of self-esteem at our disposal as fuel.

Sniff, cry, 'But I can't go back and change my childhood. Is it all lost forever if my sense of wellbeing is down in the dumps?' Nope. Even that's just a thought model, though a very fundamental and all-pervasive one. It's worth attacking as one of the first.

Exercises for more self-appreciation

Now, I (Barbel) have given many suggestions on this topic in my other books. To jog the memory of old readers and as a suggestion for new readers, here are a few old keywords plus a few new ones on how you can positively change your model for your sense of self-worth.

Mirror of love

For this you'll need a full-length mirror from somewhere. If you haven't got one yourself, borrow your aunt's, neighbour's or whoever's bedroom that's got a full-length mirror in it.

Stand in front of the full-length mirror completely undressed (watches and jewellery too) and appreciate yourself exactly how you are. Thank your body for making this life possible and put all of your concentration into sending yourself a wave of warmth. You'll see how completely and positively surprised your body and whole being react. This exercise, as well as strengthening your sense of self-worth, immensely strengthens your whole immune system.

Objective free love

The book *Leide nicht – liebe (Don't Suffer – Love)* by Werner Ablass is the number-one bestseller at my seminars and presentations. The author explains in a refreshingly simple way that you need to have a high vibration yourself in order to attract high-vibration states, such as health and happiness. It's a very easy resonance principle like on the radio: the station that I tune into is then played. But how do I increase my vibration? Easy: I love everything or consciously wrap everything that comes my way in love. What about when my horrible neighbour gets on my nerves so much that I can't love him no matter how hard I try? Also very easy: then I love myself anyway with my refusal. Then I love being annoyed and at least surround the neighbour in love. This is always suitable. And always works. The vibrations are immediately higher than when I try the impossible (loving a villain) and then feel guilty, because I'm not so enlightened.

Werner Ablass shows us, through many everyday examples of how and what, all the things you can love, so that it's always very easy and so that there are great advances in our feelings and our resonance. Decide on love and you will always feel much, much better!

For me, the book is a type of turbo-accelerator for all kinds of mental power. You can't hear any more 'radio-grief' at this frequency, because it plays at a completely different frequency.

I love my receptiveness anew.

With Werner Ablass's technique, there is an exercise that can over-come the fear of new things and the fear of failure. 'I love myself, because I trust myself to go in new directions, to take the initiative and to dare to do the unusual. This is an especially valuable quality of mine.'

If mistakes happen while doing this, there are two things to look out for. Often something new and even better than planned happens when a so-called mistake is made. The mistake was per-haps no mistake, but perhaps a sensible detour and you only judged it negatively and had fully unnecessary fear of it. And besides: 'Mistakes have nothing to do with my worth. Once they happen, I can incorporate them into my life and by doing so eliminate their negative power.' The mistake only has power over you and the abil-ity to get larger as long as you fear it and as long as you see it as negative.

Love the mistake that has been made
and thank it for its lesson
and rename it 'partial success'.

It's in this way that you remove its power and are free from fear on your next attempt. Break with the old model of having fear of doing something especially crazy or out of the ordinary that you'd normally file under 'There's no way I'd do that' and love yourself for your courage and your creativity and your readiness to try new things.

Why not try a 'nothing embarrasses me' course or give a speech on a stool in a pedestrian area. Talk total nonsense and love yourself for your courage. You'll be amazed at how many great new people you'll meet when you do such a thing at a holiday spot, for example. People in their holiday mood will be very happy to meet such an unusual, creative and funny individual like you.

Wisdom meditation

Put some relaxing music on and sit down comfortably. Just let your thoughts wander back and forth between the music and your breathing for a few minutes. When you begin to daydream or think, imagine that the thoughts are being pulled from your head and that you are returning them to the oneness of the universe. Your thoughts won't be and shouldn't be completely switched off by doing this. We are satisfied when we can reduce them a little in order for our attention to go back and forth between the music and our breathing.

After a few minutes, imagine that a small child with an enormous amount of natural wisdom and extraordinary clairvoyant abilities approaches you. The child explains to you that every person possesses a highest and a lowest potential. At our lowest potential, we live based on negative, fear-ridden and subconscious thought models. At our highest potential, we live as we really are. Free of all restrictive models, the original beauty of our being is revealed to us and we live the most beautiful and the best of what's inside us to the fullest.

It is the wise and clairvoyant child's task to see the original beauty of your soul and it's telling you at this moment what it sees! What will the child tell you?

You can now open your eyes and make notes on a piece of paper that you've already got at hand.

When the small child has finished speaking, let a wise old shaman speak. He also reveals to you, as he sees it, the whole beauty of your soul and everything that makes you a unique and valuable being.

An all-knowing fairy might follow and perhaps even God Himself as a symbol of the entirety of creation in which all wisdom and time are contained. Everything is telling you what makes you personally worthy of love.

Follow this with a half hour in front of the full-body mirror (see above) and your feeling of self-worth will take on whole new dimensions.

Ishaya's meditation

This meditation technique can be learnt in two days (very easily) and gives you very intensive self-appreciation and gratitude; see www.ishaya.com or www.ishaya.org.

Gratitude exercises from Marshall Rosenberg

Marshall Rosenberg is the creator of the really brilliant Nonviolent Communication (his book of the same name is worth recommending). There's an exercise there that contains the fuel for a positive, powerful and self-realised life. It deals with a special kind of gratitude for others and above all for yourself. I don't want to repeat it here, but anyone it may appeal to can read his book or my summary of it in *The Cosmic Ordering Service*.

Did you ever think that there'd be so many creative and enjoyable ways with which to positively change your feeling of self-worth? And there are many, many more. This is just a small part from life's infinite possibilities for recreating your life every day (think about Professor Dürr and that you've got to give yourself the chance to let new ideas have an effect on you).

Accept problems

In order to truly change something in our lives, we can't only accept ourselves as we are, we have to accept all of life as it is now at this moment.

Imagine you want to go to the Empire State Building, so you begin walking there. As long as you're in London, you'll never get there on foot. It is essential to accept what your present starting-point is. Otherwise, you'll never find your way to your desired destination.

This wisdom isn't just logical, but probably as old as humankind itself. Indian sages expressed it this way: 'Only when you're able to love everything as it is (accept what is), does the power grow within you to change anything.'

But even modern sages like Byron Katie (The Work) or authors like Werner Ablass and Rene Egli or even the spiritual teacher Clif Sanderson, who will be reintroduced below, have all always realised: the power of change grows out of the affirmation of what is.

Everything that I avoid I subconsciously feed with energy and it grows. It's like a wart that I pay too much attention to. It continues to grow. If we ignore it for a few months, it usually goes away on its own.

Or look at a child who's misbehaving. The more angry you get at its behaviour, the more it will continue to misbehave, because it is getting an amazing amount of energy and attention from you. If you ignore it when it begins to misbehave, it will quickly stop.

Putting up resistance and rejecting actual conditions cost you all of the energy that you have. It's as if you're trying to paddle up rapids in a rubber dinghy. You'll soon be completely exhausted and get nowhere.

If you're clever, you'll go with the flow and tell your life where it should go! The course that life flows through isn't set in stone. It flows as if magnetically pulled to wherever your thoughts flow; whether you want to go left or right around a rock, whether you want to set anchor and enjoy the surroundings or continue on. None of this costs you a bit of power or energy, because the power of the flow of life is carrying you.

If you believe that you are stronger than this river and want to flow against it, you will lose all of your power. And that's absurd. All the river wants to do is flow where you've told it to.

So you needn't have any fear when you accept what is. In doing this, you are telling the river of life the current coordinates where it should pick you up and to which desired new destination it should take you.

A meditation on 'Increasing self-appreciation' read by Barbel Mohr can be found on the enclosed CD, 'The Mohr Method'.

☆ ☆ ☆ ☆

☆ **Fundamental Principles of Reality** ☆

Events where people can't see
the connection
between cause and effect
are called coincidence.

Coincidence

From the situation above, we can see without a doubt that coincidence as we know it doesn't exist. Coincidence is that which happens to us. No more and no less. Every effect is based on a cause. And the root cause of all that happens to us lies within ourselves.

There's an example about host animals from biology class that I (Clemens) remember and that still deeply impresses me today:

> Host organisms are, as you probably know, creatures that are used as habitats by other organisms (also known as parasites). Now there are also parasites that 'inhabit' such host organisms for their entire life or during their development; like the little liver fluke, a microscopically small animal, for example.
>
> Its development looks like this: the small liver fluke lives in a sheep's intestines. The eggs that it lays can't develop in sheep and have to go on an adventurous journey. They

leave the sheep in its dung. The next host it needs for its development is the snail that eats the eggs.

It is here that the liver fluke leaves the first stage of its development and enters the second, which looks much different (a so-called change of shape takes place).

It is this second generation that, in order to evolve into a 'finished' liver fluke, must return to the sheep.

This second generation is separated from the snail and eaten by an ant. The organism travels to the abdominal cavity and on into the lower thorax. This causes the ant to climb to the top of the nearest blade of grass and bite into it. The ant's jaws get cramp and it is no longer able to open them. Due to this exposed position, the ant can be easily eaten by the sheep as it goes about normally eating grass.

The little fluke is then once again back where it belongs. It reaches adulthood and its final form, lays its own eggs and the game starts from the beginning again.

The next time you see an ant climbing a blade of grass, will you think it's just coincidence knowing what you know now?

There are no coincidences!
There are only events
where we can't yet see
the connection between cause and effect!

If coincidence as we commonly understand it really existed, then certainly our entire world would no longer exist. The entire cosmos runs with a precision that no person can ever imagine. Try for just one day, for example, to leave the running of your family to coincidence:

> Should the working partner or the children coincidentally come home from work and the coincidentally responsible partner or older child has coincidentally cooked the meal, then you can coincidentally eat. Assume that knives and forks are coincidentally there, otherwise you might coincidentally burn your fingers.

Absurd, isn't it?

We should guard against dismissing certain incidents as coincidence just because we're not able to understand the connections.

Everything that happens is planned!

Nothing happens by coincidence: no meeting of two people, no delays, no traffic accidents.

Everything is a part of the bigger plan.

We people shape this plan through the use of the psychic foundations described here through the kind of thoughts we have as well as through the programmes in our subconscious. We shape the plan and yet we should always be clear that we with our puny understanding will never be able to have exact control of this plan. The information and processes that are filed in our individual and shared subconscious are too complex. Our ego, which we understand as the human self, would immediately blow every fuse if it had to understand every piece of relevant data for every event simultaneously. (That's why we have filtered perception!)

Using the Mohr Method means for us: we decide on the goal and the direction by formulating a clear plan, but we leave all of the minute details of reaching the goal to the united powers of the universe and all of its so-called coincidences. You can ask just about any cosmic customer or mind programmer: the path that it's delivered on is almost always a huge surprise. You could never have imagined it in your mind. Then why grumble about it if you just have to rely anyway on the fact that the mind is too small to have the overall situation in view?!

We should see then that coincidence is the way the universe works (consciously and subconsciously) on our goals. To reach our goals, it is important to have a plan, to connect them to the cosmos and the subconscious and to trust that these two things will think of thousands more paths to reaching your goal than any mind trapped in our tiny human heads could, if only because the subconscious processes an incredibly much larger amount of data than our everyday conscious.

An example from my (Barbel's) life:
Almost twenty years ago, I had a friend from Kenya. When I recently decided to get my next au pair from an agency that works with Africa, naturally I was reminded of my old friend who was studying in Germany at the time and then returned to Kenya. I wanted (or ordered, but it doesn't matter) to find her again.

The mind with its puny ideas thought about how on earth I could do it. I used search engines on the Internet, asked at her German university and her university in Nairobi too – without success.

The mind saw no more possibilities. Then the first proposals from the au pair agency. And look, one of the girls had a very similar surname to my friend's and was also from Nairobi. 'Is it a coincidence or a sign?' I wondered and promptly chose this girl whom I already liked because of her surname. A good decision as it turned out, because the year with her went really well and the following year her twin sister came to us as an au pair.

Shortly before the change-over, the father of both girls sent me an email saying that he had run into an old friend of mine in Nairobi... anyone want to guess who it was? My old friend, of course, whom I had begun looking for a year previously. My mind couldn't come up with any effective way of finding her, but my subconscious, which is connected to everything, obviously had no problem with the matter: it pulled my attention to the right family with a small coincidence (similar surnames) and the father of my au pairs crossed paths with my friend. What a coincidence!

Brilliant, don't you think? Or, even after this example, do you still want to claim it's worth doing your head in figuring out how to reach a difficult goal? Leave the details to the cosmos. That's my advice.

Absolute personal responsibility

What do you think? How many thoughts can we consciously think at a time?

Five, ten, a hundred, a thousand?

Certainly, we've often got hundreds of thoughts going through our heads! If you were to pay close attention, however, you would see that these 'hundreds of thoughts' don't come all at once, but always one after the other. The distance between individual thoughts is only a fraction of a second, so that we could think that they all occur at once. We can only think one thought at a time, though!

And who decides what we think?

Our environment, advertising, our partners, our parents?

Of course, we're programmed by our upbringing or other people in certain respects, but when it comes down to it we decide what we think! We alone are responsible for our thoughts!

And now that we know that we can only think one thought at a time and that we alone are responsible for the content of our thoughts and when we fully see that our thoughts are responsible for our life, who makes the decisions in our lives, then? Who is responsible for us?

Exactly! We are, we alone!

So we accept responsibility for everything that affects us. In the end, we create our own world; who else should be responsible?

Everyone gets what they deserve,
but only the successful admit it.

Again:

How often do we talk about all that we've achieved, but also what we haven't succeeded in and whose fault it is that we haven't?

Whoever gives other people or circumstances power over their own lives will always live with the expectation that their own plan will time and again be thwarted.

Only when we accept total responsibility for everything that surrounds us will we have the chance to shape our future with full personal responsibility how we want it.

As long as we continue to point the finger at others and put the blame on them, we will have to wait until they change something so that we become better.

And we'll have to wait a long time for that!

With this knowledge and the understanding of the psychological basics we have drawn the short straw. I think however, that it is really a long straw, a joker on our way to happiness, health, harmony, love, success, wealth and everything else we wish for in life.

Give and take

You probably know the saying 'Treat others as you would treat yourself.'

You've most likely experienced in your own life that there's something to that.

Maybe this experience has been confirmed from different directions in that 'Everything you do comes back to you.' Maybe you read in the Bible that we reap what we sow.

If you recall these experiences again from the beginning, you'll see that it can be no other way! Let's remember:

Everything we think – and say, do and perceive – is saved in the subconscious. Everything that we do often enough and/or feel or think with intense emotion leads to a programme, an automatism. And consequently, we will automatically perceive, choose and be dealt with in accordance to this new programming.

If we behave often enough in a specific way, this behaviour will inevitably lead us to attracting people with the same programming – subconsciously, of course. And in this, it doesn't matter if the other person behaves like us or if they're just our counterpart.

An example:

Peter (17) grew up in a household where he experienced a lot of physical but also psychological violence in the form of smacks. Through these experiences – happening often and with intense emotion, of course – physical violence was programmed into him. This has led to him now trying to solve all of his problems through violence. The fact that this behaviour leads to counter-violence in his world (the others strike back), is one point.

The other is that, due to his programming, he always seeks out friends who are similarly programmed (we also know this as 'milieu'). Through his contact with other violent youths, though, he will come into contact with much more violence than if he were a part of a peaceable group. Due to this, his violent programming will become stronger and stronger. A vicious circle!

There's another point to be added here: due to his violent programming, he is also a potential victim. You remember the explanation in the chapter on filtered perception. A perpetrator will search out a victim who is also programmed for violence. It can be because the victim is scared of violence (passive) or, as with Peter, because the victim is also violent (active). This suffering from violence also confirms and strengthens his programming. The vicious circle again. This until the day that Peter changes his automatisms and begins exercises to strengthen his feelings of self-worth!

So you see, it all comes back. The example of physical violence is surely for many enlightening: of course the person who hits will be hit. Less clearly, but just as effective, this principle also works with every other pattern of behaviour.

Let's use theft as an example. Who isn't angry when their wallet is stolen? The same thing is valid here, though. Everything comes back. As consolation, you can think about the fact that the thief will also soon be stolen from!

As this isn't very helpful at the moment, think about it in another way for a minute.

If you are robbed and if for everything there's a cause, when it all comes down to the person responsible, then you have to ask yourself: when was the last time I stole something?

Those of you who have been stolen from and are also truthful people will now be – at least internally – screaming loudly!

Think about it again, though: you can also steal someone's time. Or what's become a sport in itself, insurance fraud. Did you embellish a little the last time you filed an insurance claim? Or are you one of those people who pocket the extra money when the cashier gives you – to your advantage, of course – the wrong change? There are many ways in which you – without even knowing it – can be programmed to steal.

The programming of theft (of time and other things) often has to do with the fact that you don't trust life to provide you with the things that you need. This model always leads to more shortages, though. It's like a virus of poverty that sticks to you like glue until you manage to break the cycle.

An example from my one of my lectures (Barbel):

I met someone privately with whom I had a nice conversation (perhaps better to say: tuned into) and coincidentally he was visiting the city the next week where I give a lecture each week in a bookshop. I told him that the lecture was completely sold out and that the bookshop had already turned away 500 people! It would without a doubt be full. But I should nevertheless surely with the understanding of the bookshop be able to find room for ONE person whom I knew privately. He wouldn't have to pay either. I invited him and told him I'd collect him personally at the entrance as he wouldn't get in otherwise.

What did this person who seemed friendly, but with an obvious model of the fear of not getting enough, do? He came as requested and, because I had to speak with the bookshop management, I sent my partner to collect him. That person was standing there and had impudently brought two friends and all three of them wanted to sneak in without paying. My partner was so stunned that he didn't immediately react and asked if he had misunderstood.

The three squeezed their way into the lecture room and I wondered why the woman from the bookshop was looking at me indignantly from the side. We had agreed on ONE private invitation and not three. As I still had no idea of the situation, I thought the extra two people on the emergency chairs were employees of the shop and didn't get why the department manager was so upset.

Even after the lecture, I wasn't introduced to the extra guests, but they came – uninvited just as before – with us into the café for a drink. Only when I asked them if they worked in the bookshop and the department manager rather sharply said that they didn't, even before the two could explain who they were, it was clear to me what had happened.

Okay, so it wasn't such a big deal and neither I nor the bookshop suffered real disadvantage. But the absent acquaintance suffered a real disadvantage. He had behaved in such a way – as I see it – as to not have an understanding of certain spiritual rules. He was a bit of a parasite and didn't understand what he was sending out to the world, namely his massive spiritual poverty. It's clear that I'll never invite him anywhere again when he has bitten the hand that fed him.

He rang me at home shortly thereafter and spoke on my machine saying that he had a great idea *for me* and that I *had* to ring him back. You could hear the lack of trust that life would always provide him with the right things and people gushing from every pore.

The truth is probably that he wanted something and wanted to manipulate me. By just saying 'have to', he can forget about me ever ringing him back. On the contrary: I immediately erased him from my address book.

This isn't just how I deal with things. You most likely deal with things in the same way and deal with all of life in this way too. There are often very small impulses, a wrong word, bad energy, sent out by inner automatisms with which you ruin loads of chances in life and unfortunately don't often notice, because you haven't understood the things in the mirror or taken responsibility for what you've sown.

However, when we all begin to recognise this principle of personal responsibility, then first of all our world will become more honest and peaceful and, second, our self-realisation will finally work. And the calming thing is that we don't do good deeds just for others, but for ourselves. We behave honestly so that we are treated honestly. Every deception, every lie, every unkind act is an own goal. Everything comes back to us!

You probably know of a successful businessman who accumulated his wealth through deception. And his business is going well. How is he getting it back?!

Just because we do a misdeed today doesn't mean we'll be punished for it tomorrow. It sometimes takes a while.

In such cases, though, you should take a look behind the scene. Examine the private life of this businessman a little closer, at his relationship, his family situation or even his health. I'm sure that upon closer inspection you'll see exactly where he's getting his return.

We get everything back in the end,
very often not from the person we borrowed from.

Psychological rules are always obeyed. It's often, admittedly, not entirely obvious where the cause lies. But believe me that it's there and you've created it.

But that isn't an accusation or recrimination. It simply has to do with the recognition of cause and effect. If I am clear of everything around me that I cause, either directly or indirectly, then I've suddenly got a lot more possibilities in life.

I don't have to get upset about someone who's done something to me. Rather, I can ask myself: how did I cause this? When I discover how, I can then change this spiritual setting, this behaviour, and thereby remove these causes.

If I'm always pointing the finger at others, at the bad things, and don't change my own programming, which caused everything in the first place, it will happen again and again.

And we all know that from time to time the same things do happen again and again.

An example from my (Clemens's) seminars:
A seminar participant, Klaus, has the following problem: in three weeks he's had three rear-end collisions. But, and this is what's curious, none of them was his fault. It was always another driver running into him.

Fate? Bad luck? Or just a coincidence?

Now he was open enough to accept none of these. So we sat down together and contemplated what these things were trying to tell him.

A rear-end collision is a really powerful push from behind. If he had driven faster in this situation (if this were possible for him to do), it's possible that the accident wouldn't have happened. So I asked him, 'Is there a situation in your life at the moment where you aren't making progress and where you always need a push from outside?'

Just a tenth of a second later came the answer, 'Ooohhh, yeah!'

He saw that professionally (and speaking of profession, it was a company car!) he was stuck in a dead end and wasn't ready to reach a concrete decision even though he was constantly being pushed by his wife.

He recognised that the accidents were just a result of his indecisiveness: a sign that he needed a push. Then he gave himself a push and within one day he made a definitive decision towards the welfare of his professional progress for the welfare of his family and for the welfare of his accident record. Since that time, and it's been five years now, he's driven without a single accident.

You probably know the saying that it's better to give than to receive. It's often abused even if we are ignorant of the actual reason.

You know: everything comes back to us.

Should you belong to that group of people who would rather take than give, you've inevitably got a 'take' programme. Due to your wavelengths, you probably principally attract people to you who take. You can't find anyone (or hardly anyone) who gives. So you can't take as much as you'd probably like. In the extreme, it becomes even clearer: when everyone is taking, there's no one there to give. And if no one's giving, then we've got to get it somehow. That's called stealing. But as we know, even that comes back to us.

If you want to get something, you have to begin to give. And the more people who give, the more there is to receive. Here again in the extreme: when everyone gives, everyone receives. Unequivocally.

So you can see that giving is, in fact, better than receiving. Giving is a prerequisite in order to receive anything at all.

Be careful, though! There are certain people who want to take advantage of this situation. They say to themselves, 'To get something, I have to give something in advance.' So they give. That isn't what is meant by giving, though. That's investing. You're not really giving; at the back of your head you're taking again. You always think about a return on your investment.

Giving freely is giving.
Giving is giving without expectations.
Giving is giving for the benefit of others.

This is how the principle works. Help others out of the goodness of your heart and you will be helped. Give a friend freely of your time and you will be given others' time. Give money to the needy and you will get the money back.

Even with money it is clear that the universe is designed to grow. We always get more back than we give. Great, don't you think?

Unfortunately, this is true for everything, including unfriendliness, hate or violence.

Everything comes back to us.

Another tip: don't expect to get something back from the person you've given to. Look at the shared subconscious more as a big bank, the life bank! And everything that you deposit into this bank, you'll get back. And with interest and compound interest.

Maybe not immediately, but certainly. So pay attention that with every plan and action you always keep the wellbeing of all the participants in mind. If even one person present suffers damage, this damage will come back to you. Guaranteed!

Welcome to the club

A holiday scene – beach, sun, sea, holiday club.

Who doesn't know these things, whether through their own experience or just out of a brochure?

All-inclusive price for board and lodging, including a variety of activities. From early morning to late in the night the most amazing activities take place, the most daring sports offered for free. Everyone at the club has the possibility to take advantage of whatever takes their fancy. And a good club is responsible for catering to every taste.

Of course, most guests won't take advantage of all that's on offer; you are on holiday, after all, but it is theoretically possible. Sign up if you're interested.

So you meet your fellow holiday-makers at the bar in the evening and exchange stories of your new experiences.

Someone went diving today. It was great, totally amazing. They swam through the schools of fish and even – what luck! – discovered an old shipwreck.

'Ugh,' says a neighbour. 'When I think about all of the beasts that live down there! You'd never get me down there!'

'That doesn't bother me,' says another. 'I think I'd actually probably enjoy it. I think I'll go diving tomorrow.'

This is how people talk, exchange experiences, give tips and plan their own itinerary for the next day.

Why am I telling you this? Because in our holiday club, every guest has the same possibilities as any other. Anyone can do or experience what they want, when they want. No one would think to be envious of the person who's just gone diving. Why should I? If I'm interested, I can do it too.

Every rule that is shown here is valid for every person without exception. Each one of us, no matter where we come from, our education or our relationships, is subject to these rules and can help themselves. Everyone has the same chances if they pay attention to the rules and use them correctly. We are all here in the same club. Everyone can experience, learn, achieve the same things. We should keep this fact clearly in mind:

Everyone has the same opportunities.

In the book *Chicken Soup for the Soul*, there is a case study that was done at a school in Baltimore, involving 200 youths who lived in the slums. No one gave them any chance of learning to read and write, learning a profession or escaping the slums.

Twenty years later, 176 out 180 of the youths that were found again had succeeded in all three areas: they could read and write, had learned a profession (there were even doctors, entrepreneurs and lawyers amongst them) and they lived in the city.

How did they do it? They admitted that they had their teacher to thank and the old woman smiled and said it had been very easy. She had just loved all of these kids. That gave them the power to achieve what they wanted.

Is the power of this message really clear to you? What does it mean in your life? Maybe go back to the chapter on self-appreciation, copy it down, hang it over the bed and use it daily and then you can raise a career out of the slums!

I (Barbel) was in Bangladesh in 2000 and visited Muhamad Yunus, the founder of the Grameen Bank, for a film about him there. His bank only grants loans to poor people. Those who have neither a house nor an education, and often not even shoes, are given loans by him.

I travelled randomly from village to village with the cameraman and found 'bank branches' in every second or third village. What we'd call bike sheds here, they called bank branches and they were very proud of them.

We had a translator with us and recorded a lot and talked to many people. We saw many similar results there as had happened in the study of the Baltimore slums: everyone can succeed. It doesn't matter how bad someone's starting condition is, but how good the social support that they have is and how open they are to allowing new thought models in!

This is why we shouldn't throw envious looks at those who

have what we would like to have (careful: mirror!), because everyone has the same opportunities. You need a bit more time if you're starting in the slums, but you can reach the same goal anyway!

Why be envious?

We're in the same club!

If someone has something that you'd like to have, this only means that this thing exists and that everyone can have it. We only have to apply those rules that the other person has already put into motion.

Even the most amazing achievements, the fantastic income, the biggest successes, are only possible with a club membership. And we are all, even you, part of this club.

The next time you hear that Mr So-and-so is earning such-and-such a sum, don't say like you always do, 'Oh, him! He's got this or that advantage that I don't have.'

Forget it! We're all in the same club!

Say instead, 'That's great. I never knew that that's also possible in our club!'

And if you want to achieve the same thing, then just do it. You have the possibility. Use the 'big guys' as role models who are always looking into all of the club's options and suddenly see that so many previously unseen things are possible.

Our club's brochure will continually get thicker and we may never stop adding new content to it. And every new achievement is possible for everyone else. What one person has achieved is, in fact, possible for everyone. Accessing the shared subconscious is possible for every conscious being. If we would only stop limiting ourselves, reducing ourselves, we could achieve everything we want. Look around in the world and look at those 'big boys' as a club brochure and learn from them.

The dishwasher who becomes a millionaire is really just some-one who's suddenly realised their club membership. He opened up the brochure and saw all of the possibilities. He asked reception for directions, got up early in the morning and made his way. Whenever the path seemed too long and he had doubts whether he'd ever reach his goal, he opened up his brochure and checked it. He had talked to other club members who had made the journey and told him in the most colourful details about the goal. And he knew that every member of the club had the same possibilities: he just had to follow the path.

And don't for a minute believe that in our club where everyone is equal that some are 'more equal' than others.

I've met many successful, famous and wealthy people. And all of them have the same shortcomings as we do, the same problems, the same complaints.

They're just people like you or me. And if you want to achieve what these successful people have achieved (and even more), you have the possibility.

If there was ever anyone in this world who was once ill and then healthy, you can be too.

If there was ever anyone in this world who was once poor and then wealthy, you can be too.

If there was ever anyone in this world who was once alone and then in a happy relationship, you can be too.

We are all in the same club.

We have the possibility to achieve everything in the club. Maybe not overnight, but certainly.

Welcome to the club!

☆☆☆☆

☆ **Programming** ☆

By creating the Mohr Method, we have tried to combine all the well-known and trusted methods into a simplified whole and to remove all of the unnecessary distractions, to reach the subconscious using images that delight the child within us and give it new and desirable automatisms.

In order to satisfy the sceptical side that's still alive and kicking within most of us, and because we lack experience with spiritual powers, we also want to explain the classical methods very precisely and present them as additional individual methods. Once you understand how they work from A to Z, it often becomes easier to reduce these methods to a compact minimum. If we started with the minimum, you would certainly think that we were being superficial. This is why we will start with complete explanations of each one.

Whether you use the classical methods such as visualising and affirming or the compact Mohr Method, or even a completely brand-new idea of your own which has come to you while reading this book, does not matter one bit.

The important thing is that the method you use is fun for you, makes sense to you, and that you believe in its effectiveness. Whether you end up ordering though the cosmos (as described in my (Barbel's) first book *The Cosmic Ordering Service*), reprogramming yourself, or muttering promises to your subconscious and Gaia while in a yogic headstand doesn't matter; each is just as good as the other.

There are people whose blood understandably runs cold at the silly idea of cosmic ordering. It is clear that this is not the method for them. Others fall about laughing at the idea and then sit speechless in disbelief at such naïveté. Still giggling, they make a test order and are amazed when it is delivered.

One reader recently wrote to me (Barbel) that she had been given my book *The Cosmic Ordering Service* by someone whom she had until then always believed to be totally sensible. She was very disappointed that this friend should have fallen for such nonsense. To put her friend back on the road to reason, she made two impossible orders. The first was for a parking space directly in front of her favourite bar during the evening rush hour. And what a coincidence, she was delivered this the very same evening. Well, okay, but she wasn't giving up that easily. The second order wouldn't be such a cinch for the cosmos. She drew up an extensive list of what her ideal partner would be like, and ordered him.

Her bad luck: he was also delivered promptly. Unfortunately, there wasn't room for him in her life at that exact moment, as she hadn't actually expected to get a real delivery, and 'The poor thing had to try very hard to get himself delivered,' she wrote. In the end, she changed her life around after all, accepted him and confessed to him that he had been an unwanted test order, made as a joke!

Do you know why this kind of thing actually works? Because childish, playful and truly dumb silliness opens the doors to the subconscious. You see, you can't just speak sensibly to it and then get it immediately to do what you want. Our automatisms, which usually rest on strong emotions and years of repetition, can only be unlocked and replaced using powerful keys.

Whether you believe it or not, a happy laugh can be just such a powerful key.

Now take a moment and look at the following classical techniques and the compact Mohr Method with its built-in little fun factor, and choose the method which gives you the most amount of pleasure, *now* and *today*. No one is saying that you have to stick to the same method until the day you die. If you begin to find a method boring or uncreative, or if it seems washed-up, you can simply change, whenever it feels right for you. You may or may not even want to come back to one or the other method later.

You will also come to notice your subconscious becoming more tolerant. Now, at the beginning, it wants to cling to analytical explanations and clear logic, and only allows those changes that seem possible and comprehensible to your reason.

As you become more experienced in working with yourself, as you begin to connect better with your own subconscious, it will begin to turn into a friend with whom you can chat more easily and more often and to whom you can introduce changes more easily, and with less of the hoo-ha which you are bound to experience at the moment.

Did you know, for example (sorry to all of you Barbel readers, I know that you know this example, but newcomers just have to hear this), that since the '70s, scientists have believed the physical location of our emotional memory to be in the walls of our gut? There are millions of nerve cells there, which are identical in structure to our brain cells. This is where our 'gut feeling' comes from.

The reason I mention this is that, as with every organ, there is communication between your gut and your brain. In other organs, the information only goes one way, but the special thing about the gut is that of the information passing between the brain and the gut, 90 per cent goes from your gut to your brain, and only 10 per cent from your brain to your gut.

In a nutshell, this means that our gut and our gut feeling, and so our subconscious, have far more to tell our head, than our head to tell our gut and our emotional memory.

You can learn to hear more of all of that information flowing upwards. As long as you believe that all your unconscious does, more or less, is to control your breathing, a wide range of possibilities for you to communicate with your subconscious is going to waste. You can change that, and it will change, bit by bit, with every exercise you do: for example with every exercise from this book!

1. Images

Working with our subconscious has a great deal to do with using images. Every thought that we have, everything that we hear or read, is converted in our internal 'biological computer' of a brain into images.

Some examples can explain this more clearly:

Let's look at reading first. When you read a novel and then go to see the film version, you are usually disappointed. But why? Because you have already seen it, as your own film.

When we read, we see the plot acted out in our mind's eye. As it's often put so nicely, we get the picture.

When we then see the film on the big screen, we unconsciously compare our film to the one on the screen. As our inner film is more to our taste – no surprise there, as we were the ones directing it – we usually don't like the film in the cinema.

Or imagine the following situation. In front of you on the ground is a six-metre-long plank of wood – you know, the kind of thick, strong plank that is wide enough to walk on and strong enough to let a workman push a wheelbarrow over in complete safety. This plank is in front of you, but not lying flat on the ground. Each end is supported by a brick. The distance between the plank and the ground is thus several centimetres and you know that it will bob up and down a bit when you walk over it.

If I asked you to walk along this plank, you would probably do it without giving it a thought.

Your decision to do this, however, is based on a specific reason. The moment I give you this task, you will create an internal image of yourself walking over the plank. You would decide in a split second whether you want to put this image in motion or not. If yes, you decide to do it, as in our example.

If I were now to lay the same plank between the eaves of one house and another, 20 metres up in the air, and ask you to walk over it, your decision would probably be very different. Why is this? It's the same plank, the same width and would carry your weight in the same way.

The answer is in your inner picture. In this case, your picture would show you that it wouldn't work, that you would fall. You might even already see the ambulance coming and taking you to the Accident and Emergency department.

In this situation, you judge the image to be clearly undesirable and politely refuse the offer. Of course, there is a possibility of danger here. But whether you judge a situation to be potentially dangerous or not depends on your own power of judgement. This in turn depends on your history, on your character, on your inner images.

Therefore, the only difference between the two situations is the type of inner image. If you were able to picture yourself walking over the plank in the second situation, you would probably try it. If you were able to maintain the image of success the whole way along, you would also be able to manage it without any problems.

So if we want to reprogramme our subconscious, it makes sense to do it directly, in the language that it understands, and that means with images. It is insignificant whether these images come from the so-called real world, or whether they are made-up. Our subconscious can't tell the difference.

To understand this, imagine that a screen has been set up inside your head. The images on this screen are taken and stored in the subconscious. Whether these images hit this screen from outside, through our eyes, or internally through a kind of projector doesn't matter at all. The effect is the same.

Neuro-scientists have shown objects to people in studies and at the same time measured which parts of the brain were activated. Then they asked the participants to close their eyes and picture the object themselves. The result was that the same areas of the brain were activated as before. The researchers came to the conclusion that our brains don't distinguish between real and imagined reality.

We already know this; it's like when I imagine that I'm biting into a lemon, my mouth begins to water in the same way as if I was really doing it.

As the images from our external world aren't always that positive, and we don't really want to be reprogrammed by negative realities (which we created in the first place!), we can create new internal images. The act of 'internal image creation' is what we call visualising. You can have a go at visualising now, if you want to.

Just imagine that in front of where you are at the moment, there is a little elephant. Please try to imagine it exactly in every detail.

You can see its head, its ears, its eyes, and its trunk, which the little elephant is waving about. You can also see its rear, with its tail, its legs – well, everything. Now to make things a little more difficult, imagine that the elephant isn't grey, like all other elephants, but pink.

So now you see, in every detail, a small pink elephant standing in front of you.

So this is visualising, creating an internal image. If you imagine this pink elephant often enough and with enough emotion, you will anchor this image in your subconscious and you will programme it in. This programming can be so powerful that when you next go to the zoo you will be surprised to see that they have grey elephants, instead of the normal pink ones. Are you laughing? Doesn't this happen to us on a daily basis?

We constantly have these pink elephants around us, but they have different names. We call them lazy foreigners, football hooligans, bad women drivers etc., etc., etc.

Prejudices are all basically pink elephants. Let's have a look at politics. It is incredible how differently two parties can present the same facts and so create really different points of view. Just think of the image of who the enemy is in different countries. We often have very different pictures inside our heads from how things are in reality. The images in our head, though, continue to control our actions until we change these or replace them with new images.

Imagine the little pink elephant again with a woolly hat, stripey pyjamas or with little green boots.

You will notice that by changing the picture, we also change our attitude towards it.

(Just try and change your internal picture of someone you hate. See them wearing a woolly hat and stripey tights, and maybe they will seem less threatening to you. Change the negative characteristics into positive ones and see how your attitude towards this person changes!)

One other important fact must be added to complete this programming with internal images. For this you need to try this little visualising exercise:

Now imagine that there is no little elephant standing in front of you. Don't imagine its little head and ears, its eyes and the long trunk, which, of course, it is not waving about. Also do not imagine its rear, with its tail, nor the feet and please under no circumstances imagine that the elephant is pink.

So please do not imagine a little pink elephant standing in front of you!

Did it work?

Of course it didn't. Of course you saw the pink elephant again.

We can't not imagine something!

We first need the original image in order to imagine a negative one. We know this from a variety of signs. No-smoking zones, for example, are labelled with an image of a crossed-out cigarette.

What effect does this have, though, on the programming of the subconscious?

Well, a very big effect! How do we act in daily life?

If for example, we don't want to get ill, what kind of image comes to mind? A sick bed, an operation or at least a scarf around a sore throat. As our subconscious works mainly with images, it is clear that of course the information 'sick' is registered. Your body will react, if you repeat the information often enough and with enough emotion, by becoming sick.

We certainly don't want this to happen!

We don't want to lose our jobs, we don't want to have stress at work, arguments at home, don't want to be let down in a relationship and so on, and so on.

Because we generally achieve the opposite of what we want with this 'not-wanting', it is very important for us to focus on what we want, and not always on the things that we don't want to happen.

But who actually knows what they want? Most people only really know what they don't want, and wonder why they end up getting exactly that, although this is basically a logical and completely normal thing to happen.

This is why it is called 'positive thinking', because we must focus on the positive things in life in order to make them happen. As long as I am against something, and even more so if I'm really against it, I won't be able to prevent it from happening. This is why clear and well-defined goals are an important basis for success.

We also have to look closely at the following point, in order to make it absolutely clear to our subconscious that these goals are meant for us, and not for somebody else. It makes sense that when we create these internal images, or rather films (as they shouldn't be static images but wherever possible realistic scenes) we should be at the centre of the action. Imagine yourself in the situation; imagine yourself in the environment that you wish to be in. You are the star of your film.

It doesn't matter whether you experience the scene as if you are looking through your own eyes, or if you are watching yourself from the outside. But it is often the case that if you experience it first hand, being right in the middle of the event, you give it more emotion than if you simply observe it. And as we know, the level of emotion is decisive in the speed and the strength of the programming.

Just give it a go and see which 'camera angle' is more suited to you, which option makes you feel more comfortable and choose the one, of course, that gives you the best feeling.

You can also control the level of emotion by editing your internal images. Just as in a film studio, you can brighten or darken your scenes, you can maybe add a comforting background sound-track, you can give the scenes cosy lighting to create a warm, comforting atmosphere or whatever helps you most to experience the scenes with a lot of good emotion.

Be creative! Try working with different colours, maybe with bold colours and then the next time with pastels. Do whatever you think sensible and necessary to produce your box-office hit. There are no boundaries, you are the script-writer, director and star rolled into one. You have complete control.

You can even go so far that you produce completely unrealistic pictures.

This is where I (Clemens) want to tell you the story of ten-year-old Sven, who was suffering from leukaemia.

The doctor explained to him, in a metaphor for children, that there were white and red ships sailing through his blood. The red ships are very important because they carry life-giving oxygen to the organs. Now, Sven had far too many white ships sailing about, so that there wasn't enough room for the red ships to sail by and to do their job properly. And this was the reason why he was so ill. When he heard this, he thought in his childish naïveté that if there were too many white ships, they simply had to go. So every time he went to the toilet, he imagined that lots and lots of white ships were sailing out with his urine. He had an internal image of hundreds and thousands of little white ships disappearing down the drain. Today Sven is completely healthy, although the doctors at the time had given up on him.

So a realistic image is not important for success, but rather the information contained for your subconscious. We know from our dreams that our subconscious often uses unrealistic, symbolic images. We can also use the same technique in the reverse process of programming.

Of course you should be sure to visualise exactly and realistically to achieve certain goals. We often lack the basis for this, though, especially if it is scientific or about processes in the human body. This is where the symbolic images really come in handy.

When discussing losing weight, I always recommend the following to my participants. Try to imagine that every time you go to the toilet, you lose lots of fat cells, or that every time you breathe they fly out of you. Alternatively, imagine a little digger, which is digging away at the fat cells in your problem zones. Little liposuction pipes which, in your imagination, are attached to these areas have the same effect.

So you see, your fantasy is set no limits. I'd like to give you one more good example on this topic.

If you are on a diet, and there is a piece of cake sitting in front of you, which you would dearly love to eat, do the following: imagine that all of the calories in that piece of cake are little people, who when they see that you are about to eat the cake, all rush to the furthest end of the piece in a panic. So now you can happily enjoy the front end of the piece and leave the back end, which has all of the calories in it, on the plate.

(Really hungry people can imagine that the little calorie people jump off the plate in fear, allowing you to eat the whole piece!)

These goal-images – whether realistic or symbolic – have to be programmed into our subconscious.

The best way to do this is through meditation, which I will go into a little later.

It is clear, though, that ten minutes of meditation a day viewing your internal goal-images is not going to help very much, if you spend the other 23 hours and 50 minutes sending your subconscious completely different images from outside. The images you meditate on are more likely to stick through the use of the alpha-phase compared with the images from outside, but the power of the repetition (and the probable strength of emotion you get from the actual realities) is overwhelming. Therefore, be sure that you gradually adapt your outward environment to your internal images. Of course in most cases you won't be able to do this at the push of a button, but it still remains an important part of the reprogramming.

If, for example, you want to be healthier, you should remove everything that reminds you of sickness from your surroundings. Put your medication in a drawer and put the prescriptions away. This is naturally difficult to do if you are in hospital, but do your best.

While we are on the subject of hospitals, what image do you see in your mind's eye when you hear this word? Or when you hear the words 'sick-bay', 'sick-bed', 'sick-pay'? It would be better for all of us if we had fewer sick-beds and more health-beds!

Let's look at the example of weight loss once more.

> Put up pictures on the wall of times when you were slimmer. If you don't have any of these photos, cut out some pictures of models from magazines, who have the figure you would like to have. It is even more effective if you glue a picture of your face onto the image as a montage. Hang the clothes that you want to fit into again at the front of your wardrobe: not to deceive yourself, but as a repeated signal to your sub-conscious. If you want to have more money, but you live in a poor area, go for a walk in a better neighbourhood, go and sit in the foyer of a high-class hotel, go window-shopping in expensive shops, fill-up on external riches wherever you can.

Really good external images are created if you just act as if you have already reached your goal.

> If you live alone, for instance, and want to find a partner, then just rearrange your apartment as if someone really was going to move in soon. Perhaps put a second tooth-brush holder in the bathroom, make some room in your wardrobe, or whatever you would normally do if someone was going to move in with you today.

The subject of external images also naturally includes the subject of 'television'. These images also have an effect on the program-ming of our subconscious.

I only want to make one point here, to represent all of the other ones, but perhaps the most important: violence.

Studies in the USA have shown (and elsewhere will surely not be too dissimilar) that on average every programme for adults shows eight violent acts per hour, and for children sixteen (!) per hour. At the moment, the subject of violence is the talk of every school. If we look at the facts just mentioned, this is no wonder. If we, and even more so our children, see so often and most probably with real emotion, that every type of conflict is 'best' solved with violence, it naturally becomes a fixed pattern of behaviour. Our children often don't have enough alternative images in order to anchor a different reaction. So pay real attention to the programmes you and your children watch on television; these can have a great effect on your future life. Once again: our subconscious – not only those of our children (!) – can't tell the difference between real and fictitious images.

I would like to make one more comment on the subject of images which is very important to me. As our subconscious is dominated by images, memory is primarily visual. We can see this by the fact that we find it hard to remember abstract things that are hard to visualise. So the majority of our memories are based on images. This is also true of negative situations, memories of sickness or physical injury. How often do we 'wallow' in these destructive mental images? 'Do you remember the time when he did this and that to me? When I see him nowadays, it still makes me feel sick!' and so on, and so on.

Apart from the fact that we feel sick the moment we recall this memory, the fact that we are dealing with it again naturally programmes our subconscious and ensures that the same thing happens again. *This is why it is so important that we learn to forgive.*

Not so that 'that bastard' gets off scot-free but in order to free ourselves from the negative images. There is a lot of truth in the saying, 'To forgive is to forget.'

If you still remember certain bad situations, it means that you haven't forgiven. Go ahead and forgive, stop the same old images coming back again and again.

Those who have problems forgiving – which is very understandable in most situations – should ask themselves the question whether this experience, or these experiences, weren't enough. By holding on to our anger, we only allow the same events to happen again.

Therefore once again I appeal to you:

Forgive everyone everything! For your own good.

One last thing on the subject of images:

It has become very clear to companies, especially over the past few years, that no matter how big they are even they need a goal in the form of a clear goal-image. This is why one speaks of a 'company vision'.

One has to be careful here, though, that this vision is shared by all of the employees; otherwise it will, of course, have little effect. The best way of ensuring that really everyone in the company identifies themselves with the company goal and the image it creates, is if this image is developed together by everyone. A goal that is forced upon everyone from above will never be the goal of every employee. A goal that the individual has had a hand in creating will motivate them to do everything they can in order to actually reach it.

2. Guiding principles

It is fairly difficult to walk around all day with various goal-images in one's head. One solution is to visualise your internal images every day during meditation.

Every one of us has to get through the day, and concentrating on what we are doing at any specific moment is part of this. In addition to this, the images can't work externally if we are holding onto our internal ones so hard that we overlook external opportunities to reach our goals! In the worst case, one stops seeing the external images completely because of all of the internal images, and walks straight into a lamppost!

Preparing yourself for a new goal does not mean neglecting your current tasks. Just the opposite! We should prepare ourselves for a better tomorrow through a good performance today.

Those, however, who are busy with their internal images all day long can't, of course, perform at their best. It therefore makes good sense, as one of many possibilities, to reduce these goal-images to sentences. Short, sharp sentences, which clearly describe the goal-image, are called guiding principles, or affirmations.

There are a few points to be aware of here: as we imagine our goal as being already achieved in all of our images, we naturally have to do this with our guiding principles. This means that the sentences always have to be in the present tense.

If you are ill, for example, and want to get well again, the fitting affirmation would be, 'I am well.'

You might say that you can't just claim to be well when you are still lying in bed, sick. You believe that you can't lie to yourself.

It is not a question of pretending something to ourselves. The point is that we use the way the programming of our subconscious works as effectively as possible. If we were to say 'I will get well,' we would be creating an internal image of ourselves still lying in bed, where, although we are slowly getting better, we still haven't reached our goal of being well. And you know that we always move towards very clear goal-images.

> If you say, 'I will get well,' then your subconscious will answer, 'Fine, just let me know when you have got that far!'

If you have a problem with statements that are not logically connected to the current reality, then you can also use the sentence, *'Every day, in every way, I am getting better and better.'* (This, by the way, is the oldest affirmation of modern times, developed by Emile Coué.) This gets us out of the tricky position.

If every time that you say your affirmation internally, you hear another voice telling you that none of it is true, then you won't get one step nearer to your goal. Rather the opposite, as this internal opposition comes out with far more emotion than if we say our affirmation without really believing in it. This is why you should always create your guiding principle so that it suits its purpose.

It works best for me (Barbel) when I simply think: 'I love being well' or 'Being healthy is fantastic!' This has a really good effect on my subconscious. First, there is no opposition to the fact that I haven't reached this goal yet, as I haven't said that I have. Second, I really strengthen the image of health inside me and I begin to feel the effect!

A further important basic condition for creating affirmations is to avoid all negatives. This means only using positive statements. If you say, for instance, 'I am not a loser,' you are naturally going to create internal images of situations where you have failed, and through this strengthen the programming and so cause this situation to happen again and again.

Remember the little pink elephant from the last chapter and follow the conclusions. You should, therefore, always avoid the words 'no' and 'not' in your affirmations. They don't always, but often do, have the opposite effect.

You might now have the following clever idea: if you say, 'I can't do it,' often enough to your subconscious, it won't understand the word 'not' and you will end up being able to do it. It's a clever idea, but unfortunately it doesn't work. At heart it has less to do with the phraseology than the internal image we connect it to. If we say, 'I can't do it,' we create scenes where the plan goes wrong, so once again, nothing positive. So to be absolutely safe, please try only to use positive phrases.

Your guiding principles should in my (Clemens's) opinion, also be 'short and sharp'. Many authors recommend long, strung-out, descriptive phrases. I see this as a big problem.

Affirmations are there for us to use during the day, whenever we think of them or whenever we have a clear head. By this I mean any tasks we have that don't require a great deal of concentration from us. Think of routine tasks at work or at home, think of the times when you are in the car or travelling by public transport, think about the paths you travel. How much more fun would ironing be, for example, if you didn't just do it, but with every stroke of the iron you say to yourself, 'I am thinner, what a winner!' Or when you walk down the corridor at work and say to yourself in time with your steps: 'I have the power to do all I desire.'

If your guiding principles are too long, then you often won't have the time to finish saying them in many situations. Added to this, it is the repetition that helps make them effective (or alternatively a strong emotional connection to the affirmation). If we can encapsulate our goal in a short 'slogan', we will be able to repeat it more often than a long sentence or set of sentences.

There is another reason why I am in favour of short, sharp guiding principles. We are bombarded the whole day long with negative messages. Just think of the news on television or radio, think of all of the newspapers or even of the so-called 'normal' films on television or at the cinema. We are constantly confronted with violence, criminality, illness, economic problems and other negative things. Even in everyday conversations with other people, it is often the negative things that dominate. 'Gossip' of every kind is just a representative example.

In this way we have conditioned ourselves – as you know, through the constant repetition – to think in a very negative way.

If we have, however, set ourselves one positive goal, the probability that we will continually find a heap of reasons as to why it won't work is really high.

In these situations, we can use our guiding principle as a kind of 'fly swat'. Every time that a negative thought tries to worm its way into our mind, we can counter it with our affirmation. At best, even before we have thought the negative thought through to the end.

If we have a very long affirmation, we lose this 'fly swat' function. If we first have to take a deep breath in order to say the whole sentence, the destructive thought will already be attacking our peace of mind. As we also know, everything that we think often enough tends to come true.

So that we can say our guiding principle easily as we walk along, it is good if it has a certain rhythm. If you want to make it even better, make it rhyme so that it really programmes itself in.

Some examples, which you are of course welcome to use, should show what I mean:

'I have the power to do all I desire!'
'I'm getting thinner, what a winner!'
'I am wealthy, and I'm healthy!'
'I dare to do, just like you!'
'My partner is great, our love is fate!'
'Health is best, and that's my quest!'

Or others such as:

'It's so easy!'
'I love myself unconditionally.'
'I am important!'

I (Clemens) like to combine my seminars with special external influencing factors. (When I offer something new to the outside world, I find it easier to achieve new things inside myself.) One tool I like to use very often is the mountains. I frequently go hiking through the mountains for several days with groups and make use of these external influencing factors in the following seminar.

On the subject of 'guiding principles' I regularly use the following exercise. On paths which head uphill for longer stretches, I let the untrained participants walk at first at their normal pace. The tempo is very slow, but for 'plains mountaineers' it is still pretty strenuous and tiring. Then I give them the following task: in time with their walking pace, each should also concentrate solely on saying the following sentence: 'It's so easy!' The result amazes all of them. The feeling of tiredness disappears almost completely, breathing returns to normal and all of a sudden, it really is 'so easy'!

Please try and find some of your own guiding principles, to go along with the ones mentioned here. They have to suit you and be fun for you to work with (so far as one can call it work).

In addition to taking the opportunity of saying these phrases as often as possible, you can also do the following:

Write your guiding principles on little cards or stickers and put them everywhere, especially in the places where you spend a lot of time. Stick them up on the bathroom mirror, in your car, on your desk at work, in the kitchen or wherever makes the most sense for you.

The subconscious needs a lot of impulses and, at the beginning, you will occasionally forget to work with your affirmations. This is where these little cards come in really handy.

Guiding principles are basically no different from prayers. When different religions ask for their prayers to come in the form of rosaries or prayer wheels, it is only because it is easier to programme them into the subconscious (= God) through repetition.

3. Symbols

It may be that you experience some problems saying your affirmations, or more likely, in writing them.

There you are, sitting in the middle of your open-plan office, weighing 20 kilos too much and then you go and put a card on your desk saying, 'I'm getting thinner, what a winner!' As if this wouldn't lead to sniggers all around you!

There is a way around this problem. Guiding principles are the concentration of your internal images into words. We can, however, concentrate these words even further, into symbols. A symbol can be anything that you want to link to your goal. Your fantasy should know no bounds in this respect.

One of the participants in my (Clemens's) 'Think yourself thin' seminars had created the affirmation, 'I'm as light as a feather' for herself. As her symbol she chose, of course, a feather. When she got home, she slit open an old pillow and spread feathers all around her apartment. Strangers saw it as a unique decorative style, but for her it symbolised having a good figure.

If you want a new house, use toy houses. For a car or holiday, use toy cars or aeroplanes. For health you could use a tennis ball, to symbolise your regained fitness. Of course pictures and diagrams also work; use whatever suits you.

The point of the symbol is that we come into contact with our goal as often as possible. After a while, you won't even notice these symbols any more. You will only realise that they are still there when other people ask you what they mean. But subconsciously you will link your goal to your symbol and so send a positive message to your subconscious.

4. Meditation

To make the process of reprogramming happen much faster than it normally would if you were only to follow the points above, we can use a 'turbo technique' called meditation.

Since the invention of the EEG (the electro-encephalograph), a machine used to measure activity in the brain, we have known that the brain shows various levels of activity at different times, producing different frequencies, or brain waves.

The various levels that can be measured are called levels of consciousness.

In our normal waking state, where we are interacting with the physical world around us, we produce waves at a range of 14 hertz and more. The highest levels lie at around 30 hertz, which occurs when we are very excited. The average is about 21 hertz. This phase is also known as the 'beta phase'. The level falls below 14 hertz when we withdraw our attention from the outer world and dedicate ourselves more to the spiritual. This is particularly true during sleep. Here, though, as we all know from our own experience, there are phases of deep, but also of light, sleep. It is in these light phases, where we are 'more awake', that we dream.

Sleep researchers have found out that we often move between dreaming and deep-sleep phases during the night, that we have periods every night in which we dream, and we have more than one of these periods each night. We mostly just can't remember.

These dream phases are known as REM phases (which stands for 'rapid eye movement'), because our eyes move about very quickly behind our closed eyelids as if we were watching the film that is being screened with our actual eyes.

The level at which we dream lies between 7 and 14 hertz, and is known as the 'alpha phase'.

Deep sleep lies between 4 and 7 hertz and is called the 'theta phase'. We only fall below 4 hertz when we are unconscious, and this is called the 'delta phase'.

What is important for us here, for meditation, is the alpha phase. The alpha phase is the gateway to our subconscious, when the door between the conscious and the subconscious is open furthest. This can be seen by the fact that we dream in this phase. This is when information can travel very easily from the subconscious into the conscious. When the 'door' is open, when information can travel from the subconscious into the conscious, then information can also travel in the other direction.

Now you are probably thinking, 'Great! And how am I supposed to programme myself while I am asleep?'

The alpha phase is not restricted to only the dream phase; we can also slip into this state on purpose by, for example, relaxing the body through meditation. When we are in alpha, we are relaxed, and the other way around – when we are relaxed, we are in alpha. The information we receive in our alpha state therefore leads to much faster programming of our subconscious. Everything that we see, hear, feel or even think leads very quickly to automatisms.

This is all the more important to know as we don't only reach this alpha state in sleep or meditation, but much more often.

The times just before we fall asleep, or after we wake up, are alpha phases as well. Also, moments when we are 'not quite there', when we daydream or are lost in thought. Just think about the kinds of thoughts you have at these times. Are they usually positive, constructive thoughts, or are you pondering all of your problems or things that might become future problems?

You can be certain that everything that you think about in these alpha phases reaches your subconscious very quickly and leads very rapidly to programming which will influence your life, no matter whether the contents are of use to you or not, no matter whether you want it to or not.

Levels of consciousness and age

Because of the huge importance of the alpha stage in our lives in terms of programming our subconscious, it is very interesting to look at the dependence of levels of consciousness on age.

Children and young people are particularly susceptible to the alpha phase, so that all of the information they take in leads to very rapid programming.

Just think at this point about television and video, with all of their violent scenes, of toy weapons, of the example of parents in how they deal with others and with drugs (alcohol, nicotine etc.) and other environments a child experiences such as school, friends and hobbies.

Also think of the things we tell our children day in, day out. You can be certain that very often what you tell your children will anchor itself in their subconscious and influence their lives. This is also true of the (perhaps infrequent) encouragement they get, but above all for those 'helpful tips' and all of the reproaches made when we are annoyed. With all this in mind, just have another think about the effects the following sentences could have: 'You are useless,' 'You are never going to achieve anything,' 'Life is hard,' 'Don't be so self-centred,' 'Be happy with what you've got,' etc. All of these sentences lead above all to a lower sense of self-esteem, the consequences of which are well known.

Positive and useful sentences would rather be: 'I trust you,' 'You can do it,' 'We are there for you,' 'You can't have any true wish within you without also possessing the power to realise that wish.' Just for the record: children are also programmed in theta and delta, but as these phases can't be influenced intentionally, we must concentrate on the alpha phase.

Not only childhood is important; we automatically regress to the alpha stage in old age. So everything that elderly people say and think all day leads very rapidly to programming and so becomes a 'self-fulfilling prophecy'.

Now let's be honest, how many old people do you know who have predominantly positive thoughts?

If you already belong to this age group, then take particular care to maintain a positive attitude to life. Should you have contact with older people who are dear to you, you can do them no better service than by leading them as often as possible to have positive thoughts.

My (Barbel's) grandmother is a case in point. She used to read only the headlines of tabloids and always feared the worst. When my parents were out in the car and their mobile wasn't turned on, she automatically thought that they had driven into a ditch and were dead.

After a while I stopped wanting to go to see her because she would taint everything I told her with her negative comments and fears.

One day, I had had enough. I reasoned, my grandmother is still fully mentally fit, which means that she is still fully responsible for what she says. I told her that it was no longer fun to visit her because she made all the happy things I told her negative. I told her that I would only come to see her in future if she decided to talk to me about the positive side of life instead of all of the catastrophes. And so that she would know that life had just as many positive things to offer, I would send her a positive true story every month.

From then on, until her death years later at the age of 89, I never heard another negative comment from her. Word of the stories got around to her neighbours who often popped in to ask if her granddaughter had sent another of those true stories yet.

I still remember my surprise at the elegant ease with which my old grandmother changed as if at the flick of a switch and never mentioned anything negative to me again. At the same time I put it down to the fact that she really didn't want to lose her granddaughter, but after hearing Clemens's lectures, I understood that it was because she was once again in a predominantly alpha state and that her subconscious accepted the programming immediately, which of course was highly emotionally charged. My whole family were astounded at how much my grandmother had changed in terms of her communication.

Among many other things, she no longer reproached my aunt every time she telephoned her.

Relaxing the body

In order to reach the alpha phase, we first have to relax our bodies. We can achieve this by following these simple instructions:

- You should be in a place where you will be as undisturbed as possible; that means – as far as possible – where you won't hear the telephone or the doorbell. If there is someone else around in the house, let them know, or hang a sign on the door.
- Now sit down and make yourself comfortable (if you lie down, you might well fall asleep).
- Now loosen your clothing (loosen your belt or buttons at your waist, take off your shoes, unbutton your collar, take off your glasses).
- To block out noise from outside, and also to be able to relax more easily, I recommend that beginners put on some good background meditation music. You can, but don't have to, do without external aids later on.

- Now breathe in deeply and out again several times and close your eyes.
- If you have problems keeping your eyes closed, try to rest your gaze on something that is comfortable to look at and concentrate on it until your eyes almost close of their own accord.
- It is best now to start thinking about your breathing. Monitor your breaths, in and out, without consciously controlling them.
- To support your relaxation, you can try saying the word 'relax' silently to yourself. It is most effective if you say the syllable 're-' while breathing in and '-lax' while breathing out.
- If you haven't tried these kinds of relaxation techniques before, you can try to increase the effectiveness by concentrating your mind on each part of your body in turn and saying silently to yourself, for example, 'My feet are now loose and relaxed.'

If you are still having problems after trying these techniques a number of times, we recommend that you take part in a relaxation course or autogenic training as mentioned above.

Generally, though, most people learn how to achieve bodily relaxation very quickly and without any trouble. Relaxation allows us to enter the 'alpha state' we were aiming for, in which the information we wish to transmit to our subconscious is absorbed and anchors itself particularly deeply and rapidly.

The important thing is that the state of relaxation is deep enough. Each person soon develops a feel for this themselves. Don't expect, though, that you have only reached the required state of relaxation when you no longer notice the things around you. Many people think that there must be a 'click' and that one is then 'gone' and, even better, that one should also have some sort of 'experience'. None of this has anything to do with the 'alpha phase'.

> To end the meditation, take a few deep breaths, slowly begin to move your hands and feet again and then your whole body. Stretch yourself, open your eyes and tell yourself silently that you are once more 'totally in the here and now'.

How long you spend meditating is entirely up to you – it depends on how much time you want to give yourself, on how much fun it is for you and what kind of programming you want to achieve during the relaxation. This means that you might spend just a few minutes meditating, or spend an hour or more. There is no pressure here or a recommended length of time. You will find a period that is comfortable for you and fitting for the topic you want to meditate on.

Just one final word:

The steps described here are the reason why religions ask for 'internalised prayer' and ask you to 'enter the stillness of the church'. It's just easier when you are in the alpha state!

Wishes are important signposts
to our role in life,
to our vocation.

True fulfilment and self-development
are only possible for those

who realise the wishes and goals
within them.

This is the point
of their life.

☆☆☆☆

☆ Goals ☆

Are you really satisfied with your life today? If yes, then you are in danger! Being completely happy means no longer having any unfulfilled dreams, and when we stop dreaming, we begin to die!

Robert H. Schuller

Does this sound a little harsh?

We are all taught, after all, to be happy with what we have got. We are all taught to 'touch the ceiling' and to 'play by the rules'. It is almost irresponsible to want more, given the level of need in so many parts of the world. We are taught to be humble, 'not to be so self-centred'. 'Don't set your sights too high, you could be disappointed.' In order to avoid disappointment at all costs, it is better not to have any goals at all. We have enough unavoidable disappointment in life as it is! Following your own goals is also always at the cost of others. If I want to have something, it always has to be taken away from somebody else first.

Do you know what?

Just forget this rubbish!

Forget it now!

Goals are really what keep us alive. Life only makes sense if we have goals, whether we are conscious of them or not. Try imagining the following situation:

You are standing up to your ankles in a huge muddy hole in the pouring rain on a Sunday morning. You are soaked to the skin and the earth, which you are trying to shovel out, keeps sticking to the spade. You know that you are going to be stuck here, doing this all day long.

A pleasant prospect?

I'm sure that you could think of something better to do on a rainy Sunday morning. The idea of the job doesn't exactly fill you with enthusiasm. You would probably ask me, 'What's the point?'

And this is where we come back to goals.

Now imagine the same situation, but you know that you are standing on your own property. You are preparing the ground for the foundation of the house that you have dreamed of for so long. The excavations have crumbled a bit because of the rain and the cement for the foundations is arriving on Monday. Now, suddenly, you might start to enjoy the whole business!

The situation is the same, but you see it from a completely different perspective.

There are times in life when, all too often, we are right there, in that hypothetical muddy hole. We are wet through and exhausted, and can't see the point of it all.

How often do we get the feeling that there is no logic behind certain things? How often do we notice that we are drifting through life, being pushed here and there by the current, but with no real direction, when seen as a whole?

And let's be honest: when was the last time that you set yourself goals that were really challenging? By goals I don't mean just to have a burger for lunch; they can be a bit more challenging. Goals are tasks that attract me, that I find interesting, that really create a special feeling inside me. Goals are visions, dreams whose realisation puts me in a fantastic mood.

But unfortunately we have forgotten how to have such goals.

When, as children, we expressed the desire, for the last time, to become a film star or world champion, this was probably dashed by the no doubt well-meant reply, 'You'll see soon enough how hard life is!'

Just avoid all problems, protect the dear child from failure! This is why we become increasingly 'realistic' in the course of growing up, learning to recognise dreams for what they are and to treat them accordingly, to steer clear of such 'froth'. And now here we are, as grown men and women and don't know where to go next.

I want to tell you something: *I believe that those dreams that we used to have and which still occasionally shine through, even today, are important signposts for our lives.*

This is what turns an occupation into a calling. Let these dreams be as 'unrealistic' as may be. This is where our potential lies, our chance, our life-fulfilment.

As Johann Wolfgang von Goethe put it:

> *Our desires are*
> *predictions of what we*
> *are capable of achieving.*

Take me (Barbel) for example. Do you know what profession my parents decided on for me? Head secretary. Just the thought of it still sends shivers down my spine. Not because the job would have been bad in itself, certainly not. It's a great profession, but just completely unsuitable for me. I have only had a permanent job for four months in my entire life and don't think I could stand much longer. I have always needed space and flexibility and I don't think that this really fits the job description of head secretary.

If, though, someone had said to me when I left school, that one day I would write books and would sell over a million of them, make documentaries, give lectures in front of hundreds of people and enjoy it, I would have told that person the entire set of sentences listed above: 'unrealistic, keep your feet on the ground, don't reach for the stars etc.'

All of 14 people came to my first lecture, and I took a sedative to calm myself down because I was so nervous. Nowadays I'm far more relaxed about it, even when there are 1000 people. Though I have to admit, I still use a trick. I imagine that the 1000 people aren't strangers, but my oldest and best friends, that we are sitting and chatting cosily in my sitting room, and that I am telling them what's on my mind just at that moment. There are 300 Carstens and 700 Ingrids in front of me. And I can say anything to Carsten and Ingrid, no problem...

This is why I completely agree with Goethe nowadays, that our most secret and fantastic dreams are in fact prophecies of our capabilities. There is only one thing that we can forget about. This is to plan the path to achieving the fulfilment of our dreams in advance. We really have to let this be a surprise. This in any case was 100 per cent true for me, and not just once, but over and over again. This is part of the principle: I decide on the goal and let life show me the way!

Boundaries

> *You will never be given a desire*
> *without the power to achieve it!*

Sounds good, doesn't it?

This is why I would like to repeat this sentence and ask you to take it in and think about it very seriously.

> *You will never be given a desire,*
> *without the power to achieve it!*

There is nothing pointless on earth. Take a look at the natural world. Why would there be oxygen in the air if there weren't any people or animals to need it?

In the same way, it is impossible for you to have desires without possessing the means of achieving them.

What would be the point otherwise? There is a reason for everything in the world. A reason for the existence of every plant and animal. Even when we often only realise this once we have made them extinct.

You might say that this comparison doesn't quite work with water and life. That we wouldn't have any life without water.

How true! And with the same logic, there wouldn't be any people if there were no goals. No life's work, no calling, no wishes.

So don't be so cautious in setting your goals!

Break the boundaries!

'We all live within set boundaries, which are determined by our origin, our intelligence, the law, our financial resources and our relationships. There is no way to overcome these limitations.' This, or something similar, is what we hear again and again from all sides. We are 'advised' to be happy with what little we have.

Forget it!

We are not subject to any boundaries. If we are subject to any, it is only the ones we set ourselves (or those imposed on us from outside that we accept).

Just think of all of the boundaries that were impossible to cross according to the laws of physics, from experience and everything else. These now lie far behind us.

In the men's 100-metre sprint, it was for decades impossible for anyone to run this distance in less than 10 seconds. They even found a scientific reason for this. They proved 'scientifically' that it was impossible. They argued that the laws of friction, the findings of sports scientists on the ability of muscles to accelerate and the speed of contraction, the ratio of mass to power and of air resistance all pointed clearly to the fact that it was impossible to run 100 metres in under 10 seconds. This was until a person came along who didn't believe in this scientific 'magic', shrugged it off and set himself the goal of breaking this 'sound barrier' – Armin Hary.

Nowadays every top athlete knows that this is possible and trains to achieve this faster time.

Take a look at Reinhold Messner, the mountaineer:

Before his first climb above 8000 metres without an oxygen mask, countless doctors told him that he wouldn't survive this journey, and others spoke of massive brain damage due to the lack of oxygen.

His belief in the boundlessness of human ability, however, was proved right.

Even today, he enjoys the best health and still sets off on 'impossible' adventures.

Take Hubert Schwarz, the 'Bavarian of the year in 2001':

This likeable endurance sportsman circled the earth in the year 2000, on a bicycle!

Or let's just turn to the circus:

What the 'rubber man' does is not possible purely in terms of the construction of the human skeleton. And yet he manages it.

There really are no boundaries!
Even when we try to investigate the depths of space, or the shrinking dimensions of the micro-cosmos, we have never found any boundaries other than those set by our measuring instruments.

This is often 'the nub of the matter'.

It is not the world which is limited, it is not our possibilities and it is not we who are limited, it is simply our perception. We just have to accept that there is a world beyond our five senses where there is an untold number of things that we can't see, hear, smell, feel or taste. We have been able to investigate many of these things through the development of technology, but even beyond these, there are no boundaries.

Start, right now, to think without boundaries!

Even political boundaries can only fall when someone starts to imagine their country without them. How much faith, how much force must have been behind the idea of 'thinking away' the Berlin Wall. But it worked, in spite of the most difficult of circumstances and fierce opposition.

There is another story on this topic:

A farmer at the market was selling a pumpkin that was shaped exactly like a jug. When asked how he had been able to grow a pumpkin in this form, he replied that he had put a jug over it when it was small. The pumpkin then grew into the jug until it had filled it completely and then it stopped growing – what else could it do? At harvest time, the farmer smashed the jug and was able to bring his prize to market.

We, too, often have a kind of jug placed over us in terms of our limitations. This means that we can only ever grow to a certain size and form.

I (Clemens) often use the metaphor of a garden fence, which surrounds us and restricts our freedom of movement. Remember, you can push back the fence as far as you want to. You might even want to throw it out altogether.

Fight against every kind of limitation – be boundless. If you start to cry out from within yourself, to protest against this lack of boundaries, I understand completely. We all grew up with 'boundary-thinking'. If you now say to me that one has to be realistic, I can also understand. But think about how 'realistic' the great thinkers and scientists in history were. Was flight realistic for people in the Middle Ages? Was it realistic to transplant a human heart into a stranger's body? Was it realistic that the Berlin Wall would fall?

'Real' is for us the things that we can 'real-ise'. We are limited, however, by our five senses, the technical possibilities and of course by our filtered perception. There are naturally things which we can't change so easily, but these are tasks which we would not usually set ourselves to change (at least not unless it really was a deep personal desire)

Have the courage to make the 'impossible' possible!

The 'impossible' is much more possible than you probably think. To prove this to yourself, you can do the following exercise. It is designed to test the maximum stretch of your upper body and your tendons:

Stand somewhere where if you stretch out your arms you have space all around you without touching anything. To prepare for this exercise, first turn your upper body gently to the left and then to the right, keeping your feet fixed to the floor. The movement should only come from the hips.

Now do the following: stretch your right arm out in front of you at eye level and point your index finger, as if you were pointing something in the distance out to someone. Now turn your upper body, with your arm outstretched to the right. Your feet, of course, stay fixed to the floor. Look along your index finger the whole time as if you were aiming a gun. When you have turned as far as you can, remember the spot you are pointing at with your finger. Repeat the exercise a second time. Now that you are warmed up, you will probably get a bit further than the first time. If you think that you can get even further, then repeat the exercise a third time. You will now have found out the maximum stretch of your upper body. Take another look at the spot you were pointing at last, the furthest you can turn. Now choose another spot that is further past your maximum, a spot that is a good bit further, a spot, which according to the maximum stretch you have just discovered, would be impossible to reach.

Close your eyes and just imagine – without actually doing it – that you repeated the exercise and were able to reach even the new point.

And now really try the exercise again. Start from the same position as before and turn your upper body to the right.

Almost every participant with whom I (Clemens) have done this exercise was actually able to reach this supposedly unreachable new point. This is proof that there really are no limits, other than the ones we set for ourselves.

Analysis of potential

If you want to, this is where you can discover your personal potential – ideally for all of the important areas in your life in one go. It stands to reason that our lives should be supported by more than one pillar. In my (Clemens's) opinion, they should rest on five pillars.

Professional life

This pillar includes your career, but also your calling and your life's work. Many career-oriented people make the mistake of supporting themselves on only this pillar. Everything is arranged according to the needs of their profession. This often leads to them having success in their professional life but not in the other areas.

Finance

Of course, we earn our money though our professions, but we should give particular attention to the area of finance. Many people regularly spend more money than they earn and then wonder why they never seem to be able to save. It is all the more important to think about our finances nowadays as practically no one can count on getting a pension that will allow them to maintain the living standard to which they are accustomed. I would like to refer you at this point to the relevant literature in the appendix, in which the areas of money, capital investments and long-term investments are covered.

Relationships

Partners and the family are most important in this area, but also friends and colleagues. We have to nurture our relationships to keep them alive. It is easy to neglect personal relationships, especially if you are career-oriented. You stop nurturing your partnership, thinking, 'Well, I'm already married.' But just like a muscle that you don't look after, that you don't train and use, it will waste away. Think of a leg that emerges again after being in plaster for six weeks: partnerships that aren't nurtured can waste away in exactly the same manner. Of course, it isn't possible to invest the same amount of time in a relationship as in, for example, your profession, but it is more about focus, attention and simply being aware and actively nurturing it.

Body

This deals with health, looks and the figure. Interestingly, modern medicine has discovered that the human body is designed to live for an amazing 120 years. The precondition for this is the correct nutrition, enough exercise, doing without poisons such as nicotine and too much alcohol and having a positive outlook on life. Many people treat their cars better than their bodies. Many people use their bodies as if they had a replacement lying around at home. It is also now known that the reduction in performance of the body has less to do with advancing age than with the wrong care and treatment.

Development

This means learning about new things, further education and even simply developing your personality. When things stop growing in nature, they die. When a tree ceases to grow, it dies. Even for humans, there are things that keep on growing. We certainly don't get taller, but our fingernails and hair keep on growing throughout our lives. In the same way our mind and spirit grow inside us in a wholly natural process. We have to make sure that we actively support this process through developing ourselves.

If we actively maintain all five pillars, our lives will rest on solid foundations. If there are five pillars, then one is allowed to become a little wobbly from time to time. We still have the other four to carry us forward. Those who only have one pillar, for example their profession, will understandably give up very quickly when they have problems in this area. It also makes sense that each individual pillar relies on the others, that one can see them as joined together at the bottom.

It is similar to our hands: we all have five fingers but if you hit one of your fingers with a hammer, you don't just say, 'Never mind, I still have four.' It hurts really badly. It is like this in life. When there is a problem with one pillar, all of the others are generally affected. This is also why we should pay equal attention to all areas of our lives.

This is the basis for working ecologically and economically. Ecologically, not only in the sense of 'in harmony with nature', but in the sense of 'for the good of everyone involved'. Just remember, what goes around, comes around. Therefore, only do things that help everybody.

Economically means gaining the most amount of return for the minimum of effort. The method, which we are describing here is, in my opinion, the best way of automatically reaching our goals with the least amount of effort.

Life can be divided into three basic areas: being, doing and having. In our society, most people first want to have something, then do something, and then, through this, be someone. Only, as we so often experience, it doesn't work out like this. We have to start with being: to create a new image inside ourselves, in our psyche, a new goal-image. Then from this inner being, this inner consciousness, we will act differently. Having will then follow automatically.

As you can see, the goal of everything that we do is, purely and simply, happiness. If you ask yourself why you want to have certain things, to do certain things, to be something – if you ask yourself often enough, 'Why, why, why?' – you will answer in the end: to be happy.

The goal of all of our effort,
all of our actions,
is, in the end, happiness.

When we found our lives on these five pillars, when we set ourselves goals in each area, then happiness becomes more and more a part of our lives.

Now we come to the analysis of potential.

You will see various forms to fill out on the following pages. The first ones have the headings: Being, Doing and Having.

The first: ask yourself what or how you would like to *be* for each of the five areas of life: profession, finance, relationship, body and development.

The second, what you would like to *do*; the third, what you would like to *have*. Each, once again, for each area of life.

Just remember: our wishes are signposts for our abilities. What we are, do or have therefore has a lot to do with our potential. These lists are not just about writing things down that are realistically possible from where we are today. (Think about the section on Boundaries!) The idea is that you list all of your desires. What you do about them later is completely up to you.

NLP (neurolinguistic programming) became particularly well known through the three project rooms that Walt Disney is said to have had. He used the first room for wild and limitless fantasy about what he would like to do. In the second room, he asked himself what he would need to put all of this into practice, and only in the third room did he allow the critic inside him to voice doubts. Armed with the list of what was necessary and the critical comments, he marched back into the first room to think his vision through again.

In this way, Walt Disney repeatedly made possible what had been technically impossible in the film industry.

The trick is not to let your visions be mangled by the critics too soon, as then nothing new will ever be created.

The fourth list is titled: Things that I can do well. Naturally, these are also signposts to our potential.

Just think about the things you really can do well, and this 'do well' does not have to be how everybody else would term it.

Let me give you an example:

Our colleague Vera F. Birkenbihl once told us that she used to really suffer from the fact that she spoke too much when she was younger. She suffered, because she wasn't invited to any parties and her peers actively avoided her. One day, one of her uncles took her aside and said, 'Just let me say two things. First, who is that complains that you talk too much? Is it those who don't say anything themselves, or is it those who would like to say a lot themselves, but don't manage to get a word in edgeways when you are around?' And it was, in fact, more the second group of people.

And for the second point – and this was the important one – he said, 'The ability to say a lot in front of groups of people, being able to say something to others at all, is a wonderful gift, a potential that many people don't possess.' And that is when it all became clear to her. Nowadays she gets paid well for talking so much.

So once again: things that you can do well won't always be seen that way by everyone.

One more important point: don't tell yourself that you can't do anything well. It doesn't have to be anything fantastic. Being a good listener can be a wonderful ability. Running a household and bringing up children are of immeasurable worth.

The last list is titled: Things that I enjoy. Just think about the things that you really enjoy, which make you happy, which make you blossom. These are also clues to where our real calling lies.

When you have filled out these lists, have a look to see if there are any main points that jump out from all of the things you have listed. Maybe you will find new headings, new goals in which the others suddenly fit. These can then be categorised into life goals and calling.

Being

How/What I would like to be! _____

Profession: _____

Finance: _____

Relationship:_____

Body:_____

Development:_____

Doing

What I would like to do! _____

Profession: _____

Finance: _____

Relationship:_____

Body:_____

Development:_____

Having

What I would like to have! _____

Profession: _____

Finance: _____

Relationship:_____

Body:_____

Development:_____

Things that I can do well

1. _____

2. _____

3. _____

4. _____

5. _____

6. _____

7. _____

8. _____

9. _____

10. _____

11. _____

12. _____

13. _____

14. _____

15. _____

Things that I enjoy

1. _____

2. _____

3. _____

4. _____

5. _____

6. _____

7. _____

8. _____

9. _____

10. _____

11._____

12._____

13._____

14._____

15._____

Your own personal goals

When you have filled out these forms, when you have found headings, if you honestly didn't restrict yourself, then you should have a fairly good overview of the things that you want to achieve in life.

What you don't yet know is which of these desires reflect your personal life plan, and which were imprinted on you from outside in the course of your life.

Try to do the following:

Sit yourself down and relax (as if you were going to meditate) and experience your wishes coming true. (This is the same exercise as with re-programming, but has a different aim here.) Take each point one by one, and see yourself after you have achieved it. Act as if it was already a fact. Go into every detail, experience everything that is connected to this goal.

You will also be forced to see things that aren't so positive, that you missed in your initial enthusiasm. Try to consciously look for these negative aspects. What didn't you think about when you conceived this goal?

This simple exercise can show you all of the consequences connected to your goal. We often forget (or choose to forget) the negative sides of things. But you can only decide whether or not you still want your wish to come true after you have weighed up all of the advantages and disadvantages.

It is certainly classy to drive a great sports car. It certainly has its good sides, which one always sees, underlined by advertising and by society. If this exercise has shown you, however, that you have to go to the petrol station every 400 kilometres and spend a lot of money there, if you have seen bills for insurance and taxes suddenly appear before you, if the costs of service and repairs make you feel queasy, then you have all of the information you need to make your decision.

If a goal really is a personal goal, something to do with your life's work, with your calling, you won't be able to find any negative sides or, if you do, you will be able to accept them knowingly.

As soon as you have had some practice in putting your wishes down on paper, in categorising your wishes, you will notice the following happens:

When you become aware of a desire, you will picture it already having come true. In this moment you will experience the feeling that you have probably experienced so often. You will understand whether the fulfilment of this desire satisfies you, if it is worth the journey and the effort, or if it isn't a real, personal desire.

In this way, you will be in the position in the shortest time to be able to differentiate between 'true' and 'false' desires and so steer your life ever more quickly in the direction of your calling.

Goal – not path!

In setting your goal, make sure it really is only the final goal, the end result that you have set your sights on. Our logical-rational upbringing makes us tend towards choosing paths. As soon as a goal comes to mind, we ask ourselves, 'But how should I get there?' and we reject the whole idea outright, though we can't see all of the possibilities with our – relatively speaking – limited powers of reason.

So you should try to visualise the goal and not all of the steps necessary to reach it.

If your wish is for a house, then just keep imagining that house, in all its detail, as if you were already living there. Don't picture the money you need for it, the credit, the deposit, the builders or anything else that is part of the path.

Just act as if all this had already happened – at least in your imagination. There are so many paths leading to your dream house. More, maybe, than you can dream up yourself.

Here are two little examples of how life finds its own path, from readers of *The Cosmic Ordering Service:*

Christel from Wilhelmshaven wrote the following to me (Barbel):

'My husband, my son and I live in Wilhelmshaven and once wanted to drive to Fantasialand in Brühl. As we didn't have much money, I sent an order off to find cheap places to stay. We drove off and stopped at a car park by the motorway, just before our destination. There was a car parked in front of us with a number plate from Cologne. The couple in it started a conversation with us and told us that they had just come back from Wilhelmshaven and were driving to Cologne. As we were chatting and asked them how best to get to Brühl, they told us to follow them and if we wanted, to come and have coffee at their house. We did this, and while we were drinking coffee, they asked us if we already knew where we were going to stay. When we replied that we didn't, they suggested that we stay in their guest bedroom for the night. We were pleasantly surprised, because they seemed so friendly. That evening they invited us to dinner, so we got a wonderfully cheap place to stay and a new friendship, which is going strong, even today.

Everyone I tell this story to finds it difficult to believe, but I assure you, that this is really what happened.'

People who obstinately refuse to be imaginative would in this case have probably brushed off the pair from Cologne, reasoning that they didn't have time to go for coffee because they still had to find a cheap place to stay…

This is where many deliveries are hidden by life, behind nice little events and sometimes behind little detours.

Example 2: Mrs Pommerenke has her own wonderful little Ayurveda practice on Lake Wörthsee. Customers are really spoiled there and also get high-energy massages from her. She also has three children. That the occasional thing doesn't always get finished at home is understandable. She thought that getting a cleaner for her flat would be too much of a luxury, so she just shot an order off to the cosmos, into the blue, for a helping hand at home once a week, which if possible wouldn't cost her anything.

Unbelievable but true: this order was delivered. A customer told her soon afterwards that her daughter was at a household management academy and was looking for an internship in a private home, once a week. She was supposed to cook, clean, tidy up and so on, unpaid – in return for a bit of help and direction. She had actually got a good home-help for a year completely for free.

So how does this kind of story normally come about?

You have a desire.

You check out the possibilities and come to the conclusion: no money!

And that's it!

Never ask for what you can get. Your subconscious is far cleverer than you are. Just tell it what you want.

This simply 'saying what you want' is a central point.

The only thing – and we mean this in all honesty – that you really need to do in life is to tell your subconscious in a way that can't be misunderstood what you really want to have.

The Bible has this to say about this point:

Ask and you shall be given.
… knock and the door shall be opened.

But you still have to ask for it!

You still have to knock!

Of course this isn't the end of the matter, but it is the basic pre-condition for success. If you don't say what you want, then you can't complain if you don't get it. If you don't decide where you are going, others will do it for you. If you don't live your life yourself, it will be lived for you.

For this reason, listen to your inner voice, listen to your desires and tell them to your subconscious. Every day! The next chapter will tell you ways of how to do this. Then your subconscious will automatically steer you in this direction.

Naturally you have to walk the path yourself, but you have already gone a little along the way. Up to now, you have always been steered by your upbringing in the ways in which you act, your body and your perception.

Now you have set a course that will guarantee you happiness in life, fulfilment, success, health and all the other things you desire. You can't expect, however, that if you set off for your goal today you will already know all of the twists and turns along the way. Many people don't set off at all, because they don't know 100 per cent of the way in advance.

There is a kind of 'corridor principle' in life. Imagine that you are standing in a long corridor, in a school or official building. You are standing at the beginning and see various doors off to the right and left but the further you look along the corridor, the less clear it becomes, and you can't quite make it out. Only when you start walking along the corridor will you realise that there is maybe another corridor, a stairwell or even a lift. This is to say that the possibilities only become clear further along the way, possibilities that you were unable to see from where you stood at the beginning.

This is exactly what happens in life. We first have to set off before we can see our possibilities. We have to take the famous 'first step', to 'get the ball rolling' and will only then see all of the opportunities that we can make use of and that can help us along the way. These useful opportunities are usually not visible from where we stand today. Be courageous and off you go.

Taking the first step

Taking this first step is of central importance. Studies into successfully concluded projects have shown that the first step must be taken within the first 72 hours – that means the first three days – for the project really to have a chance of success. So if you set yourself a new goal, think of a first step that you can take within the first 72 hours. It doesn't have to be much. It could be a phone call, a chat with someone, even ordering a catalogue. The most important thing is that you do something to move in the direction of your new goal. This is first to give a sign to your subconscious that you really are serious. On the other hand, it is one step down the corridor that can open up new possibilities which you hadn't thought were there until then.

And another tip:

Keep your goals to yourself at first, as long as you are still a 'beginner' in using this method.

Of course, people who will be directly affected by your goals should be informed in time. (If your goal is, for example, to emigrate to Canada, then you should at least talk about it with your partner first!)

The reasons for this 'keep-it-to-yourself' are the following. First, we are surrounded by so-called 'givers of good advice'. People who, without meaning it badly, want to protect us from bad experiences.

So if, full of euphoria, you tell everyone that you want to lose 20 kilos, those around you might talk you out of it very quickly. 'How do you think you are going to manage that?', 'It's a pipedream' or all of the other well-meaning pieces of advice.

The other thing is that change is not normally appreciated by those around us. Others have got used to you the way you are. If you change yourself, they might be forced to change themselves as well. (Maybe then they wouldn't have an excuse to be fat themselves any more!)

Good advice – when you look at it more closely – is often only good for the person giving it. I don't want to say that you should never ask for any advice again, or that everybody only wants the best for themselves.

I want to give you the chance to gain your own experience with this, without any prejudices. When you have reached your goal other people will come to you themselves and ask you how you managed it. Don't let yourself be talked out of the opportunity of really achieving your goals. Try it out for yourself first. You can only gain.

The second reason for you to keep your goals to yourself initially is the following:

If you set yourself a goal today (let's stick to the example of losing 20 kilos), then you might change this goal later. We all change constantly, and our goals change with us.

While you are working on this issue, you might realise that the problem isn't your figure. Maybe you used to think that you could only be a complete person by being thin, but now you have learnt to develop a new sense of self-worth and you are content with your figure.

But you have promised everyone that you were going to lose weight and in the face of concerted opposition you might have said out loud, 'I'll show them all that I can do it.'

Now you are caught in a vicious circle, and you might end up pursuing this goal not for yourself, but for others. But then you aren't living your life for yourself, but again for others. And you actually wanted to put an end to this kind of remote control!

How programming works

In order to understand programming better, imagine that a tube exists in our subconscious for every topic in which we can store information.

Every thought, and with that of course every word, every action, every perception and every feeling, is placed in the relevant tube. None of this information is lost. The tube starts to fill up. When we have reached a certain level, the contents of the tube will be automatised by the subconscious. We then have a new programme.

As there are tubes for every topic, this means that there are tubes which contradict each other. So we have a tube for 'being fat' and one for 'being thin' (or even one for every stage in between, but for the sake of clarity we will stick to the simplified model here).

The automatic processing occurs for the tubes which contain the most content, that means the ones we fill up most in the course of our lives. This is why people with a figure problem have the feeling that they have occupied themselves with the subject of 'being fat' more often, and with more emotion, than with the topic of 'being thin'. As the tubes for 'being fat' have more content, your automatism will be steered by these tubes. (All of those affected know how automatically this actually happens!)

So if you want to switch the programming to the 'being thin' tubes, you have to keep putting information into the 'being thin' tubes for so long that there is more information in them than in the 'being fat' tubes.

We get this information, as already discussed, either by repeated or emotionally charged new input, or through programming carried out with a feeling of lightness and feeling of natural-ness in the alpha state.

By using the first method, which is often an easier technique for the beginner, you have to repeatedly work with the subject of 'being thin'. Every time, however, that you waste a thought on 'being fat', this will of course be saved in the 'being fat' tube, so that it will slowly be catching up.

The same goes for feeling. Since we said that the stronger the emotion that is connected to a piece of information, the quicker this leads to programming, we can look at the following model.

Each thought has a particular 'value' which raises the level in the tube. The larger the emotion that is connected to a piece of informa-tion, the higher the level in the tube is raised. Repeating the guiding principle *'I am thin'* ten times indifferently could have the same effect (and so the same value) as a single frustrated *'I am much too fat.'*

This is the explanation of why it makes sense to remove the real causes of an outside symptom.

If, for example, you are overweight because you are scared of bodily contact, then the information coming from this will raise the level of the 'being fat' tube. If you want to reprogramme using only your 'being thin' tubes, you can do this by thinking about 'being thin' more often and with more emotion than 'being fat'. However, since the cause hasn't been addressed, the information will keep going back into 'being fat'. The reprogramming that you have already achieved (the 'being thin' tubes being fuller than the 'being fat' ones) is thus reversed.

The same basic process happens with the 'nearness' and 'dis-tance' tubes. As the automatic process is set to 'distance', information will repeatedly be processed – automatically – through this channel. The setting must be changed to 'nearness'. This then works according to the same principles of repetition and level of emotion.

If 'nearness' is transmitted from now on, this will be one of the sources of information that automatically fills the 'being thin' tube.

In parallel with the reprogramming of the root causes, we have to integrate our goal in our programme. As the 'being thin' tube generally has more catching-up to do we have to use all of the ways already described to switch the automatic setting to this area.

This is where another important point comes into play. As long as the information going into the tubes has no big bugs, the process will prove to be unproblematic. We can calmly let the programming process take its course. As soon as the existing settings are 'threatened', as soon as the 'being thin' tubes reach the critical level of the 'being fat' tubes, the existing automatism starts to defend itself. It will do all it can to save the current setting. (This is in itself a good mechanism, as what good would an automatism be if it gave up its job at the first sign of a problem?!)

We usually experience this 'self-defence' as thinking of giving up. The setting tries to manipulate us very cleverly and to convince us that 'the whole thing is pointless' or that 'it never works anyway'.

So whenever you become frustrated while programming, when you want to give up, it is a good sign. It shows you that you have almost reached your goal. Now you have to keep going, to make a greater effort. If you stick at it now, you have won, then the old programme will no longer run automatically. You will be steered by a new automatism, but now one that you really want to have.

✩ ✩ ✩ ✩ ✩

☆ The Mohr Method ☆

We have divided the Mohr Method up into differing styles: Yin and Yang.

Yang is the male power, the power of clarity and the sun, but also the power that is wonderfully logical and reasoning. Yin, on the other hand, is the female power, the nebulous power of the moon.

I (Barbel) have followed the meditation techniques of a spiritual teacher who updates his method every year with very complicated but very precise details. At one stage he made it known that there were 113 techniques for activating the body's own energy fields. 112 were very precise and always done in the same way. They were all Yang, or male techniques. The 113th technique was female, Yin, and completely chaotic. It changed every day and simply followed its whim in whatever was most effective on that particular day!

We both also want to give you the possibility, through the Mohr Method, to programme yourselves absolutely individually. This is why there are different building blocks, a Yin way and a Yang way. You can choose a method according to your personal view of life and always stick to this, or put something new together every day, according to what feels most up-to-date, or you can even choose a mix of the two.

If someone asks you what exactly the Mohr Method is, then you can tell them this:

'The queen of all metallurgies, as it contains both Yin and Yang.' Or: 'A kind of mental building block system!'

Let's turn to the first, the male method.

The Yang technique

Choose a goal you want to reach and make the following plan:

- First write down your goal, in all of its detail.
- Think of an image that speaks to you. This means create your goal-film. Think exactly about what the result should be – not the path there. Create a real script. (The detailed vision of the final result is also important, so that you can really tell when you have reached your goal. The individual details are therefore also criteria to know that you have arrived.)
- Reduce your film to a fitting guiding principle. Describe your goal using short, sharp, succinct words.
- Reduce your guiding principle further into a symbol and spread this around in all possible and maybe also impossible places.
- Choose a place and a time in which you can practise your daily meditation. The best thing is to set a fixed time for meditation in your daily routine – just like eating or cleaning your teeth.

Now do the following:

- Sit down at your accustomed time and place for meditation and relax yourself.

- Now let your goal film run before your mind's eye in all of its detail. If it is short, you can replay it several times.
- Be certain to experience the film with as much emotion as possible. You can ideally allow a smile to appear on your lips while meditating. Just enjoy having achieved your goal – at least the vision of it.
- Now say your guiding principle silently to yourself while continuing to watch your film. (This enables you to form a strong link between your goal-image and guiding principle.)
- Now let your symbol appear in your film. (This anchors your symbol firmly to your goal.)
- Now let the voice inside you fade out, let your film and symbol fade away slowly, bring your programming to an end.
- Breathe in again deeply, begin to move your body again and open your eyes. Ideally the good emotions that you created during the meditation will remain with you for a long time (in the best case until the next meditation).

In addition:

- Say your guiding principle to yourself as often as possible in the course of the day (either out loud or silently to yourself!).
- Change your surroundings as much as possible to reflect your new goal! (Put up pictures of your goal, rearrange your home, visit places where you can see and experience your goal.)
- Spread your symbol all over your home!
- Pay attention to your words and thoughts! These should always be directed towards your goal!

- Try to surround yourself with positive people, who support you.
- Make a plan of action. You know your goal. Divide the bigger goal, where possible, into smaller goals and work towards these in turn step by step. (If your goal, for example, is to move abroad, it might be necessary to learn the language first. You can start with that today.) Important: you should still only visualise your final goal during meditation!
- Take responsibility for reaching your goal yourself. Always ask yourself, 'Is what I am doing at the moment bringing me any closer to achieving my goal?' If not, just stop it. If yes, carry on!
- And the icing on the cake (for advanced practitioners): always ask yourself, 'If I could be certain of reaching my goal, what would I do then? How would I behave? How would I act? Today?! Now?!'

And then go ahead and do it!

On the subject of faith

Everything we have discussed here is not a newfangled programme or technique that you can either put it into practice or just forget.

Since you have been on this earth (and this begins in your mother's womb) you have been programming through the power of your thoughts, through your perceptions, your words and the things you do. Only you don't usually know it, you don't have a clear idea that it is happening. This simply means knowing the way the programming works, understanding this and beginning to put it into practice in a conscious and targeted way.

Faith is always mentioned in the context of mental programming. Every world religion is based on faith. The Bible itself says that faith moves mountains. (By the way this old book teaches all of the spiritual laws mentioned here in a wonderful, though mostly coded, form.)

For us, faith is the inner certainty that the goal that you set yourself will actually become reality. This means that there must be a clear understanding between your logical rational thought, your consciousness and your subconscious programming. The contents of the conscious and subconscious are in this case identical.

As this identicalness, as we have seen, is called up through constant repetition and/or strong emotional attachment, we can't believe in certain things unless they are firmly anchored in our subconscious.

So when we identify new goals, if we want to give a completely new direction to our lives, then we can't start off by believing in them. If I learn as a child that 'I will never achieve anything,' and if I manage to make the prediction come true more than once through my programming, then I won't be able just to start believing that I will achieve something wonderful.

Faith can only start to grow when we have internalised the new information.

What is most important in doing this is less the faith in achieving your goal than the discipline of actually carrying out the reprogramming of the subconscious in the way that we have set out.

When you have achieved it, you will believe in it. At the latest when you can see the results with your own eyes.

The only thing that could possibly influence you in terms of faith is if you don't have faith in what we have described here. If you are of the opinion that the whole thing sounds really good, that the odd thing might in fact be true, but it is certainly not for you, then you won't even try it out in the first place. Why should you? It won't, in your opinion, work anyway.

Do yourself a favour, though, and just give it a try. At first with small things. Then when you realise, to your surprise, that it does actually work, then you will believe that you will be able to achieve everything else in the same way.

I (Clemens) know that you really can achieve anything. I know that when something is anchored in your subconscious, you will believe in it. And if you believe in it, you will achieve it.

The Yin technique

Initial thoughts on the Mohr Method with added fun factor

Neither of us (neither Clemens nor Barbel) is a member of a church or religion. Nevertheless, we keep quoting from the Bible. If we had grown up in a Buddhist area, we would have quoted exactly the same things, albeit in a slightly different way from the local texts. The great thing to see is that all of this knowledge has always been around in every realm and has always been adapted to each culture and for each new generation.

You can read, for example, in the Bible, that we should try to be like little children. Anyone who has read this book carefully can have a good guess at why. Aren't children generally in the alpha phase, that phase we should all try to reach in which the subconscious is particularly susceptible to reprogramming and accepts reprogramming so quickly?

We as adults have to take the, certainly enjoyable, time for meditation or use the time in the morning just after we have woken up to profit from this alpha phase.

Or, something which also works, we become as the little children by becoming more playful, less serious, happier and lighter, more cheerful, more loving, more open, more trusting. This brings us closer to the alpha phase in itself, as we automatically start to relax completely when we let ourselves fall into childish, cheerful and happy play. Relaxation immediately produces the alpha phase.

You won't be doing anything silly, but something that has been scientifically proven as sensible, if you build your own fun factor into your programming technique for your subconscious.

But please observe your own reactions to this. If you don't enjoy what you are doing, but still feel silly, then please use the classic individual method, or the Yang style, of Mohr Method.

If you notice yourself becoming happier and more relaxed using the Yin style, or you've invented a method with your own in-built fun factor, then this is for you. You must always take yourself seriously and start at the point where you find yourself at the time in terms of your relationship to mental powers of every kind. Be kind to yourself! Think of the effects of high and low levels of self-respect. If you feel the need, go back at this point to a previous chapter and find the exercise you need before you decide how to carry on programming.

(Useful/necessary) warm-up exercises
Composting or packing things away in the Easter Bunny's cupboard

Normally it makes the most sense to steer your attention towards the things you would like to have and simply overwrite the old programme instead of feeding the old, which you are trying to get rid of, by giving it new attention.

Suppressing it is no help at all. Whenever you have the feeling that an old pattern wants to be examined again and won't allow itself to be overwritten until that's happened, you can use this part of the Yin-style Mohr Method as a warm-up exercise.

The only thing that you need to do this, while you are relaxed, is a clear purpose. Relaxation brings you into the alpha phase and raises the effectiveness, as we already know.

You can start by going through the short meditation exercise as described above to relax yourself, or any other exercise you know. The main thing is that you are relaxed.

Now all you need is a clear sense of purpose in order to take an old pattern of thinking that has popped up, and either compost it, or pack it away in the Easter Bunny's cupboard.

Just a little diversion on the subject of the effectiveness of clear purpose. A healer that I (Barbel) know told me recently that he had flown to Hong Kong to learn acupuncture. The specialist, however, told him that he had arrived too late. The healer didn't understand what he meant, until the Chinese homeopathic doctor explained to him that it was no longer fashionable to stick needles into patients. One had found out that it was not the needle, but the intention of the healer that drove the process. Nowadays one spreads all of the needles out decoratively, to impress the patient, but the treatment itself was only carried out through lightly touching and relaxing the patient and the intent of the healer to activate the relevant points on the meridian lines (meridians are the energy channels which run through the body, the basis for traditional Chinese medicine).

You have just as little need to torture yourself with needles or to over-exert yourself in order to shed your old thought patterns. If you have a clear purpose and an internal image that you enjoy, while you are in a state of relaxation, your subconscious will accept this from you and happily store it.

As soon as you notice a thought pattern which isn't compatible with your new goals and shows itself to be resistant to attempts at positive reprogramming because it wants to be looked at again, the Yin-style Mohr Method gives you two possibilities: you can compost this pattern, or pack it away in the Easter Bunny's cupboard.

The Easter Bunny's cupboard

To put it simply: you probably believed in the Easter Bunny at one time, didn't you? Even that was a thought pattern. You are quite happy to remember it, but it has no influence whatsoever any more on your system. The pattern is archived, but switched off.

If you become aware of old thought patterns, which you no longer want, you can switch these off and archive them in the Easter Bunny's cupboard in just the same way.

You can even go so far as to slip into a toy shop next Easter (unobserved and undercover in a hat and coat, naturally) and buy yourself a pretty box and a sticker of the Easter Bunny. You then write all of the thought patterns, which you no longer want to have, on little cards or slips of paper and pack them away in your own personal Easter Bunny's cupboard.

Composting

If the Easter Bunny's cupboard isn't really your thing, there is a second option.

Put all of your old patterns, or patterns which no longer fit your new guiding principles into the composter or simply on the compost heap. This has two advantages: the patterns are immediately robbed of their power to do harm and secondly get a new use as they are broken down and become fertiliser.

'What you fear is what you get,' as they say. What you fear is what you are usually most attached to. Fears are highly emotionally charged thoughts, and therefore powerful. If I know that I can take the unwanted automatism and simply put it in the composter, close the lid on it and that it will rot and break down into fertiliser, the emotional fear goes away very quickly.

You can even build yourself a nice box for this purpose and paint it green or brown (perhaps like the composter in your garden, if you have one) and put the patterns you are going to compost in there.

Each time one of those unwanted thoughts pops into your head, you can reach for the mental fly swat, which in this case is, 'Oh, that's just one of those patterns that is mouldering away in the composter… that's right, go on mouldering away!' This swat instantly takes all of the fear energy out of the thought. It no longer has any power over you. How could it anyway, if it is just starting to rot and break down into compost?

You will know when the pattern has finished composting because you will no longer notice it.

It will never pop up again and is almost erased from your memory. It might come up again under hypnosis, but is otherwise completely gone.

Dieter M. Horner, one of the trainers at the Barbel Mohr Academy (as, of course, is Clemens), has another wonderful method. He changes the old thought pattern into a very similar new one and affirms the new version, as described above. The subconscious then thinks that it has been making a mistake for years and has just remembered the wrong pattern.

Examples:

From
   'I never achieve anything'
make
   'I always achieve something.'

If
   'Humbleness is a virtue'

is stopping you from stepping into the limelight and making more of yourself, then change it into the new guiding principle:

'Loving yourself without pride is a virtue!'

as this is much closer to what the principle was originally trying to say.

From

'No one ever calls me'

make

'Thank God no horrible people ever call me, but lots of great people call me and I call them!'

And so on. The contents of every one of these old principles can be reformulated with a little bit of fantasy.

Thoughts on reprogramming using the fun factor

As we have seen, we can, if necessary, compost old thought patterns or pack them away in the Easter Bunny's cupboard.

Now we have to prepare the soil for the new ones, so the new seed can grow and thrive as quickly as possible.

For this, I (Barbel) would like to tell you the story of the New Zealand teacher Clif Sanderson. He worked for five years in the children's hospital in Chernobyl. While there he treated children with a technique he had developed called DFR (deep field relaxation). The Russian Ministry of Health even awarded him the Gulperin prize for services to medical science for his work.

When Clif arrived, 12 to 15 children were dying each week as a result of the reactor disaster in Chernobyl. After just one week of his treatment, the numbers of children dying each week dropped to 3!

In addition to this he himself wasn't affected or showed any rise in radiation levels in his body, although he lived, worked and ate the contaminated food of the region for five years.

How did he manage it? Let's hear what he has to say. Clif Sanderson on DFR:

The field which I work in is the field of creation, the whole field of existence, and is also the field in which all of the information of the cosmos and of all time is stored. It is the only thing that is truly real in the whole of the cosmos. Matter is an illusion, as modern physics itself now recognises. All of us live in a kind of information soup, and are part of it.

To understand this properly, we have to enlighten our ego. The ego tends to oppose life and constantly to say 'no' to that which is. In addition, it also wants to know everything very precisely.

Let's say that you were suffering from a chronic illness and you consulted doctors and healers because you wanted to be 100 per cent certain of the causes of your illness. Then it could easily be that one of the doctors told you that the cause of your illness was too much stomach acid. The next might say that it could be parasites, while a third says a virus. Yet another might tell you that it was caused by an unre-solved experience from your childhood which is having a physical effect on your body. Completely depressed, your trudge over to the next practice where they are convinced that your gut and digestion are at the root of the problem.

Now who is right? Maybe they are all partly right, but what is the absolute prime cause of the illness? Where should you start? The truth is: no one knows. No ego knows it or will probably ever know it. The cosmic field of all-knowledge knows it, however. It contains everything and thus knows it. It is also the best contact partner for the highest power of transformation and complete healing.

So what can we do? We teach the ego to stop continually opposing the flow of life and to say 'yes' to life, instead of 'no'.

This will relax our ego and we can relax more and more deeply with our whole being. We can relax so deeply that we connect again with the field of creation and can trust that it knows what is best to do.

All of nature tends towards harmony, as Einstein himself knew.

DFR simply trusts this natural tendency.

When we look at the results of the research which we have talked about in this book, then we can see certain similarities, although the perspective is a little different here.

By relaxing we enter the alpha phase of brain activity. Every purpose which we formulate in this alpha phase reaches our subconscious and is stored there.

All of our 'subconsciouses' are part of a greater whole, which we can call 'the field of creation', 'common subconscious', or whatever we choose.

If many fears sink into our subconscious, they become truths for us and affect our lives. We magically attract the things that we are constantly afraid of.

So if we want to avoid or reduce global and personal catastrophes, then it certainly makes sense to let our happy trust sink into our subconscious and let it grow there!

If you leave your individual subconscious while programming and intentionally place your goals in the common field of wholeness, then the pull towards realisation will be maximised. This means it is almost unstoppable. 'But,' you might well ask, 'if everything is interconnected anyway, then doesn't each programme automatically end up in the whole?'

You are right; well noticed. The difference is rather that our conscious communication with the cosmos intensifies when we turn our mind to it on purpose. It is never the case in life of whether the cosmos is listening to us, but whether we are listening to the cosmos. By turning our attention to the fact that we are connected to this larger field, we notice it much more. The energy follows the attention. It is just like autogenic training: you also get the warming energy in your right hand (for example) by turning your attention purposefully towards it.

If you live your life and think as if there were no connection between yourself and the cosmos, then you simply won't hear what the cosmos is telling you.

You should see it as a kind of soil, which you prepare by including the possibility of being helped by the cosmos in it.

An ever-growing number of 'crazies' out there call it 'cosmic ordering' when you let yourself be consciously advised by the cosmos, but you are welcome to see this as too silly or weird. This is exactly what the Mohr Method is for.

The natural state of the human being

Maybe you have already realised that the natural state for humans is health and self-fulfilling happiness in all areas of life.

How else would you explain that all unharmonic feelings disappear immediately when we relax our entire bodies and all of our muscles? Human nature is to be happy.

This is why there is a main affirmation in the Yin-style Mohr Method, which is:

My nature is to be happy

This includes health, calling, positive relationships, completeness and enjoyment in development.

You can write this sentence (with or without the accompanying explanation) on a beautiful piece of paper in gold paint, or whatever suits you best, or even create a complete painting around it or ask someone to paint it for you. Hang the painting in your bedroom so that you see it every day when you go to bed and when you get up (as you already know, because of the alpha phase just before you fall asleep and after you get up).

This also prepares the soil for the growth of your seeds.

As nothing can be done in the entire universe without love and thankfulness, you should take the chapter on self-appreciation seriously and select one or two of the exercises in it to prepare your fertile soil.

The last part is very easy, the part where you connect to the field of the whole and engrave your new goal on it.

And how can we do this?

The first piece of good news is that, even here, simple clarity of purpose is enough. While you are doing your meditation relaxation exercises, simply imagine that your spirit shoots out into space and connects to the network of energy that surrounds the earth, then you can deliver your goal programme to it and let it flow into the whole.

You can also imagine that your heart is connecting to the heart of the cosmos (the cosmos doesn't need a physical heart, one of energy is enough) and your order is transferred from heart to heart.

This means you have intensively programmed into the collective subconscious, not just into your personal subconscious. As your personal one is by far the smaller one, it will automatically do what you have informed its boss, the collective subconscious, should be done.

Dr Shioya of Japan uses a very similar method, which also works by placing goals into the universal whole. He is over 100 years old and still winning golf tournaments for pensioners, although he was born in poor health. His wife, who uses the same technique is 96 and just as fit.

The second piece of good news is that you don't have to constantly repeat this. The all-knowing has good hearing and a good memory. Just do what God did in the Bible: send your goal into the wholeness for six days and make the seventh day your personal Sunday. Celebrate, treat yourself.

The bigger the goal you send in, the bigger the programme of spoiling yourself on the seventh day should be. Go to a scent, sound, oil and super-enjoyment massage, to the opera with your best friend or whatever you really enjoy and really relaxes you.

And then? Water the soil by dedicating yourself to self-appreciation in your daily life. Get the best and the highest quality out of your current daily life. Don't tell me that it is bad. Think of the slums of Baltimore and of Bangladesh, think of what people can make of their lives if they want to and integrate love.

The rest will take care of itself – usually in the most unexpected ways. But only if you stick to it and keep watering your soil (= self-appreciation and making the best out of your current daily life).

I have been speaking of the good news. Is there also bad news? Well, half bad. The first piece of bad news is that you can't programme any bad goals into the network of the common subconscious (also seen as the all-oneness or the big whole). That is to say, you can, but you had better get the bag of ice ready now for the slap that you will receive in return.

Just remember: it is human nature to be happy! And you come along and want to programme bad luck? Forget about it. One can only fabricate bad luck if you turn far enough away from the all-oneness, not when you turn towards it. You can't get any more darkness into a room by turning on the light.

If you want to be absolutely sure that your goals fit your nature of happiness and all involved and that they won't turn to dust because they were dark, then just include this in your programme: '… so that it is for the good of all!'

How the all-oneness then manages it isn't your problem. A single person can't possibly be as creative as the big whole, in which all knowledge of all time is held.

The second slightly bad piece of news is that the method is powerful, great and proven to work (you can read all about the 100-year-old Dr Shioya in the book *Dr Shioya's Fountain of Youth*). However, this is a catch, when you know it: it works far better when two or more people put it into practice at the same time and programme the universal spirit of the subconscious for each other as well. They don't even need to know what goals the other person has. It is enough to use a code word or code number for the goal and to use that.

This means that you need people on the same wavelength if you want to try this out. To do this you will have to admit that you think that this 'rubbish' has some truth in it. Oh dear, oh dear.

May I suggest something to you? It is good if both of you have an interest in programming together. Why don't you set one of your first goals as finding the perfect partner to programme with?

And when this person appears, then you will know at least that the method works and now you can really set to work together and support each other. For six days. Don't forget. You don't even have to be in the same place. It is enough if you agree beforehand in a quick phone call what you are supposed to be programming for each other and then if possible meditate at the same time (you can ask for your wishes first, your subconscious will be glad that you are putting yourself at the centre, and your partner can do exactly the same).

It is of course even better if you live in the same area because then you can share that seventh day, your personal programming Sunday, which can just as well be a Saturday or any other day of the week.

In my (Barbel's) 'ordering' seminars, we always make use of this effect in that everyone always programmes for everyone else, or rather orders. This means that it is not quite so individual, and you are never sure what you are ordering for the others (other than that one can attach 'for the good of all') but there are many reports of far faster results than if you programme, code, order, manifest or whatever all alone.

Do you still have questions? Go ahead and ask. This book was written for sceptical people, after all. It isn't clear to you why it works so much better with another person or group of people? Good question.

There is an interesting experiment with monkeys on this subject. A monkey was placed by itself in a cage and then subjected to sudden loud noises, light effects and even shaking the cage. The monkey reacted with (who would have thought it?) utter panic.

As soon as two monkeys were put in the cage and given the same nasty surprises they also reacted with fear, but not as much as the single monkey.

If one put a whole group of monkeys in the cage, say five, and frightened them in the same way they reacted not with panic, but with only a slight interest in the events.

The same goes for people. We are social animals, and when we are together in a group, we are automatically able to relax more fully (and so reach the alpha phase). We also take comfort from the presence of others and feel stronger for it and are not so easy to frighten or to be shaken by anything.

Anyone who has meditated both alone and in a group will know that one can usually relax more easily quickly and deeply in the group. As the saying goes 'you can't pick each other up off the floor', you have to support each other. Apart from the purely physical side of life, one can also help each other at the same time to 'pick yourself up off the floor'.

On the vibration plane, you all help each other to vibrate at a higher frequency than before.

The placebo effect is also well known (pseudo medicine). A placebo works much better if the doctor prescribing it thinks he is prescribing the real medicine than if he knows it is a placebo. His expectations rub off onto the patient. In exactly the same way, we can create a positive field of expectation for others and so increase the effects.

Before you choose either the Mohr-Yin or Mohr-Yang Method, you should already have a feeling for which one makes you feel better inside.

What is absolutely clear is that we steer our lives with subconscious automatisms. What is clear and unchallenged is that children accept thought patterns most easily because they are mostly in the alpha phase. From this it is also unchallenged that relaxation is an important factor for reprogramming. Whether you achieve this through pure meditation, autogenic training or the rediscovery of your childish side, with a lot of fun and laughter, or whether you simply programme before falling asleep or just after waking up because you are close to the alpha phase at that time, is up to you.

An overview of the Yin-style Mohr Method with built-in fun factor

- Relax in the way that suits you best.
- Pack your old thought patterns in the Easter Bunny's cupboard

or decompose them in your composter. Try to really imagine how the pattern starts to rot and finally is broken down.

- On top of this, if you want to, you can reformulate your old thought pattern into a new one that sounds similar, but has a completely new and positive meaning. You should ideally write this one down and use it as a new affirmation.
- Prepare the soil for the seed of your new thought pattern.
- Make a work of art out of the sentence 'The nature of human beings is to be happy' and hang it in your bedroom, so that you see it as soon as you wake up.
- Once your subconscious has really absorbed this message, it will move you more and more in this direction, every time you relax, without you even having to think of your end goals!
- Preparing the soil, part 2: As nothing big happens in the whole of the universe without love and thankfulness, you should treat the chapter on self-appreciation seriously and select one or two of the exercises to use in preparing your fertile soil.
- Programming into the big whole:
- Relax yourself and imagine that you are flying out into space with your spirit, up to the network of energy that surrounds the earth and contains all of the knowledge about everything that has happened on earth. Or send your wishes from your heart into the energetic heart of the cosmos. Let your goal-image sink into this energy network with the parting words '… so, for the good of all'.
- Repeat this every day for six days and on the seventh, celebrate your personal programming Sunday by treating yourself to something particularly good and special on this day.

- If you find the right person, you can carry out this exercise together or in a group. Simply place both of your goal programmes in the common subconscious through your spirit journey. Imagine that it will be really easy for your partner to achieve their goals.
- Water your new goal-seed by getting the most quality out of your current daily life. You can do this best through self-appreciation and thankfulness and consciously living for the moment.

☆ ☆ ☆ ☆

☆ Quality Programming ☆

We are now kitted out with all of the special turbo-programming techniques. 'What should we choose first?' you might ask yourself, with happy expectation. Many people first programme career and money.

Or try something a little wiser: 'calling' instead of 'profession', which means fulfilment in doing – and career only if this comes out of it by itself, and all of this in financial comfort.

Okay, so that is clear for the first round. But as with Mohr-Yin, for example, programming only takes seven days, so you could choose a new topic for next month. What should it be this time?

We would like to remind you at this point of the chapter about the five pillars: standing on one leg isn't so easy! These programming techniques work and sometimes people get carried away by their success (usually men) and think that nothing can stop them now and in their gold rush they forget about the other pillars. In these cases a rapid rise is often followed by an equally rapid fall and a hard landing on the floor. If you become completely unbalanced as a person and a living thing, because you concentrated on only one pillar, it means that you have programmed your own downfall, as the universe only reflects what the person is really like inside.

This is why we would like to give you a few tips for further rounds of programming. How about the following:

- 'My body is completely healthy.'
- 'Spiritual, mental and complete bodily health.'
- 'I am a good mother/father.'

Instead of 'I am going to programme myself a new girlfriend / a wonderful new boyfriend, who is like this and that,' it is more efficient to programme the following:

- 'I am the best boyfriend that anyone can have.'
- 'I programme myself to have this or that characteristic.' (a characteristic that one would want a good friend to have.)

I hope that you realise how great the last two programmes are. What help is it to you, to programme the best new partner when you send out the signals of a workaholic or send out the signal of having a tiny sense of self-appreciation? It will never work. The person you're looking for won't want to have you.

If, on the other hand, you programme yourself to be the best boyfriend that anyone can have, then this will have an inevitable effect on your inner qualities. You will send these signals out and inevitably attract others with these qualities.

> *I recognise my friend,*
> *who doesn't want to entertain either me or himself,*
> *but just wants to sit there.*
>
> *Jean Paul*

Programme yourself to be this kind of friend. This is the best insurance against too much stress in life.

The same with the programme: 'I am a good father' or 'I am a good mother.' If you believe the opposite and send these signals out, your children will always feel neglected, even if you are there for them round the clock. Send out 'We are wonderful parents.' Then you won't have to be there for nearly as much time, and the children will still feel 'satisfied' by the quality time you spend with them. What it comes down to here, as in many other areas of life, is quality and not quantity.

And: you won't be able to fall into the trap of becoming a workaholic because the automatism you have set yourself (of being good parents) will work against it. Without you thinking about it logically, you will spend time with your family and, what's more, you'll enjoy it.

With the subconscious automatism: 'I am a useless father and never take care of my children,' you can even put the times when you are with your children into your appointments calendar, and it still wouldn't get you anywhere. Something would still probably come up every time, or just when you wanted to go and play with the children you will get very important phone calls which will keep you busy for hours.

If you change the programme, the conditions will be exactly the other way round: you wanted to work late, but were finished surprisingly early and since it is so hot, preferred to go to the swimming pool with the children anyway. And suddenly no one seems to call any more when you are just about to jump off the five-metre board or throw a water bomb!

Further themes for programming might be:

- 'I am physically fit and full of vigour.'
- 'I am enjoying my personal development.'

I know a lot of mid-sized entrepreneurs who have told me that they definitely wanted to be millionaires very quickly. Not a lot happened apart from stress and frustration and lots of work, so in the end they gave up. They saw that life is too short to spend it working madly and under pressure to perform.

The new goal was suddenly that everyone should be happy, the employees, the customers, and the family at home above all. How much they earned from this was suddenly no longer important. They wanted quality of life.

All of a sudden it got around that theirs was the best and most enjoyable place to shop, or that their service seemed somehow to have an aura of good humour around it. Sometimes this went so far that the top employees of their competitors resigned to come and work for them. The staff were hardly ever ill any more and everyone performed better, in spite of less overtime and more communal tea-breaks.

Short and sweet: all of a sudden they were richer than they had ever been before, or even millionaires and hardly knew how it had happened.

They had turned from being a stork (one-legged and one-pillared) into a millipede (standing firm on every pillar) and this had its effect on their income.

A Mohr Method programmer wants everything, but one pillar

alone will not do it. Be excessive and optimise your programmes in every area!

Which method is the right one for me?

Should I choose the Yin or the Yang method, and how far do I have to stick to the details? What is right for me?

Relax, you can decide yourself, because it doesn't matter!

It used to be that a guru would sit on a red velvet cushion and say that if one wanted to programme one's subconscious, one could only do it in this way or with that and in any case one had to be certain to do this and that.

The more we have learned, the clearer it has become to us that the most important thing about the whole process is just to understand that it is possible. This is what we have tried to present in this book as logically and comprehensibly as possible.

The rest, how you actually go about reprogramming, is relatively unimportant. It has been proven that one reaches one's subconscious more easily in the alpha phase, and it is certain that rituals of many kinds can help in this (a certain repeated procedure is also a kind of ritual). But the more often you communicate with your subconscious, the clearer the path becomes. As soon as you have experienced that it works a few times, your subconscious will start to listen more quickly and more effectively.

Most of our subconsciousnesses are not used to being spoken to directly let alone consciously reprogrammed. This means that it might be taken aback at first, or overexcited or even a bit mistrustful, who knows.

The more often you communicate with it, however, the more it will trust you. You might even be able to do without alpha, rituals and all that comes with it sooner or later. You might then be able to be having a shower, set yourself a clear new goal and that'll be it.

Cosmic ordering (as in Barbel's first book *The Cosmic Ordering Service*) is just a super-turbo short form of the Yang or Yin method in this book.

It may be that you need something that is easier to understand for the scientifically oriented part of your reasoning to get you started, or that you get the feeling that cosmic ordering might work for the little things in life, but that more attention must be given to the 'important' things in life.

Do you know what? As soon as you think this, it becomes a fact.

The Mohr Method should therefore be understood as a building-block system that one can arrange individually for oneself. The first step to creating a perfect connection to your own subconscious is to feel which facet of the programming will get the best response. How can I convince myself best at this moment? That's what I'll use.

- It might have occurred to you that the whole ritual of reprogramming is a little bit inconvenient if you are just hoping to get a parking space in the congested town centre, a suitable wedding present in a hurry, to get through the supermarket check-out quickly, have nice customers straight away or something similar. I don't want to have to reprogramme for days just for this. See it as your homework to put together a quick version from what you have read here for just these situations. Three recommendations for an absolute beginner follow. You really should try, though, to become your own guru when it comes to finding out how your personal communication with your subconscious works best:

- The super-fast turbo method, which probably works because of its slightly absurd and childish approach, is cosmic ordering. Even if I can't stop myself from praising the advantages of this method, it doesn't mean that you have to go out and buy the book. You can find lots of free tips on this on my homepage www.baerbelmohr.de (the website is in English as well as German).

- Remember the flow of life in the Problems chapter? Pass your coordinates on to the universe through your thoughts and choose where you would like to get to: 'Attention, I'm in the town centre, on the main street. I am going to be in my favourite café in five minutes, please let me flow past a parking space on the way.'

- Important: don't row against it (i.e. complain and repeat a thousand times that there won't be a parking space, otherwise your flow of life can only let you flow past full spaces).

- Really far-out people think that we live in a field of endless possibilities and only determine what is currently visible in 3D through our consciousness and our observations. You can reprogramme with: 'Freeze [freeze the unwanted situation] and fade away [fade out slowly]! I teleport out of the field of endless possibilities the following into my three-dimensional experience here and now:…'

Just remember: as soon as you know and have internalised the fact that it is possible, the way to it is secondary. Choose the method that you can believe in most at the moment and which feels the most powerful to you personally!

You are the creator of your own reality and you can define the way in which you want to create yourself! This is the first step, and a very important step, to getting very close again to the power within you.

See yourself with new eyes
and you will become a new person!
Reinvent your life!

Why don't you decide which automatisms are allowed to enter your system instead of letting others decide for you!

Peace, happiness and everything you wish for yourself,

From Barbel Mohr & Clemens Maria Mohr

☆ ☆ ☆ ☆

☆ About the authors ☆

Barbel Mohr was a photo reporter, photo editor and graphic designer; she started writing as a hobby in 1995. Her first book, *The Cosmic Ordering Service*, was first circulated only among her friends as a photocopy until it found a publisher in 1998. By 2005 a million copies had been sold, and so far *The Cosmic Ordering Service* has been translated into 12 languages – which has surprised no one more than the author herself.

She began to give seminars and lectures in 1995. In 2000, she produced her own video (*Fulfilling Your Heart's Desire Yourself*), and bore twins at the end of 2001. Since then she has reduced her public appearances.

All you need to know about Barbel can be found online at www.baerbelmohr.de.

Clemens Maria Mohr is one of the top German business trainers and currently only available for training courses open for the public through the Barbel Mohr Academy. He has been working for 15 years in this field and is one of the few great Motivation and Mind trainers with this length of experience. He is a qualified sports doctor and mind trainer. His customers include multinationals, mid-sized enterprises and sports clubs such as the German Ski Federation. Clemens Maria Mohr has co-authored *News from the Dream Catching Angel* in addition to *Cosmic Ordering for Beginners*. He is the author of many other books, CDs and cassette courses. His website is www.clemensmariamohr.de.

☆ Further Reading ☆

Carroll, Lee and Tober, Jan:
- The Indigo Children; Hay House, 1999
Griscom, Chris and von Rohr, Wulfing:
- The Healing of Emotion; Bantam, 1990
Hay, Louise:
- You Can Heal Your Life; Hay House, 2002
- Heal Your Body; Hay House, 1994
Hill, Napoleon:
- Think and Grow Rich!; Aventine Press, 2004
Lundin, Stephen C., Paul, Harry and Christensen, John:
- Fish! For Life; Hodder Mobius, 2004
Mohr, Barbel:
- The Cosmic Ordering Service; Hodder & Stoughton, 2006
- The Cosmic Ordering Guide Book; Hodder Mobius, 2007
Molcho, Samy:
- Body Speech; St. Martin's Press, 1985
Murphy, Joseph:
- The Power of Your Subconscious Mind; Ariston, 2002
Patel, Dr Mansukh:
- Mastering the Laws of Relationships; Life Foundation Publications, 1997
Peale, Norman Vincent:
- The Power of Positive Thinking; Vermilion, 1990

Ponder, Catherine:
- Dynamic Laws of Prayer: Pray and Grow Rich; DeVorss & Co., 1987

Redfield, James:
- The Celestine Prophecy; Bantam, 1994

Robbins, Anthony:
- Unlimited Power; Pocket Books, 2001
- Awaken the Giant Within; Pocket Books, 2001

Rosenberg, Marshall:
- Nonviolent Communication; Puddle Dancer Press, 2003

Scheele, Paul R.:
- The Photoreading Whole Mind System; Learning Strategies Corporation, 1999

Schuller, Robert H.:
- If It's Going to Be, It's Up to Me; HarperSanFrancisco, 1998

Schwarz, Hubert:
- Power of Mind; Suedwest Verlag, 2002

Seiwert, Lothar J.:
- Balance Your Life; Piper Verlag GmbH, 2004
- How to Simplify Your Life; McGraw-Hill Contemporary, 2004

Sheldrake, Rupert:
- Dogs That Know When Their Owners Are Coming Home; Arrow, 2000
- The Rebirth of Nature; Inner Traditions Bear and Company, 1994

Sher, Barbara:
- Wishcraft: How to Get What You Really Want; Ballantine Books, 2003

Silva, Jos :
- The Silva Method; Souvenir Press Ltd, 2000
- The Silva Mind Control Method for Business Managers; Prentice Hall, 1994

Tompkins, Peter and Bird, Christopher:
- The Secret Life of Plants; HarperCollins Publishers, 1973

Tracy, Brian:
- Maximum Achievement; Simon and Schuster, 1995

Waitley, Denis:
- Innovative Secrets of Success; Simon & Schuster Audio

Wenger, Win and Poe, Richard:
- The Einstein Factor; Nightingale Conant, 2000

Yunus, Muhammad:
- Banker to the Poor; PublicAffairs, 2003
- http://www.grameen-info.org/

☆ ☆ ☆ ☆

☆ Hay House Titles of Related Interest ☆

If You Could See What I See, by Sylvia Browne
The Amazing Power of Deliberate Intent, by Esther & Jerry Hicks
Ask and It Is Given, by Esther & Jerry Hicks
Angel Therapy, by Doreen Virtue
I'd Change My Life If I Had More Time, by Doreen Virtue
Messages from Your Angels, by Doreen Virtue
Spirit Messenger, by Gordon Smith
The Unbelievable Truth, by Gordon Smith

☆ ☆ ☆ ☆

☆ Notes ☆

☆ Notes ☆

☆ Notes ☆

☆ Notes ☆